CU00663348

The Maurya Empire

A Captivating Guide to the Most Expansive Empire in Ancient India

© Copyright 2021

All Rights Reserved. No part of this book may be reproduced in any form without permission in writing from the author. Reviewers may quote brief passages in reviews.

Disclaimer: No part of this publication may be reproduced or transmitted in any form or by any means, mechanical or electronic, including photocopying or recording, or by any information storage and retrieval system, or transmitted by email without permission in writing from the publisher.

While all attempts have been made to verify the information provided in this publication, neither the author nor the publisher assumes any responsibility for errors, omissions or contrary interpretations of the subject matter herein.

This book is for entertainment purposes only. The views expressed are those of the author alone, and should not be taken as expert instruction or commands. The reader is responsible for his or her own actions.

Adherence to all applicable laws and regulations, including international, federal, state and local laws governing professional licensing, business practices, advertising and all other aspects of doing business in the US, Canada, UK or any other jurisdiction is the sole responsibility of the purchaser or reader.

Neither the author nor the publisher assumes any responsibility or liability whatsoever on the behalf of the purchaser or reader of these materials. Any perceived slight of any individual or organization is purely unintentional.

Free Bonus from Captivating History
(Available for a Limited time)

Hi History Lovers!

Now you have a chance to join our exclusive history list so you can get your first history ebook for free as well as discounts and a potential to get more history books for free! Simply visit the link below to join.

Captivatinghistory.com/ebook

Also, make sure to follow us on Facebook, Twitter and Youtube by searching for Captivating History.

Contents

Introduction

For nearly a century and a half, the Maurya, or Mauryan, Empire existed as the largest ancient empire on the Indian subcontinent. Stretching from west of the Indus River Valley (modern-day Afghanistan) to include the rest of the Indian Peninsula, except for the southern tip, Maurya was a geopolitical and cultural phenomenon. In 321 BCE, the Maurya Empire was established by the ambitious and well-connected Chandragupta Maurya, who controlled a network of loyal followers through his mentor and chief advisor, Chanakya.

After about a quarter of a century of uncontested rule, Chandragupta was followed by his son and heir, Bindusara, who reigned for around twenty-four years. In 268 BCE, the determined Ashoka (*Asoka*) controversially rose to power, supposedly by murdering several of his brothers. After Ashoka extended the boundaries of the empire, most notably through the conquest of the Kalinga region, he unexpectedly turned to the non-violent path of Buddhism and spent the remainder of his thirty-six-year rule spreading the Buddhist religion to the far reaches of the Maurya Empire. Ashoka's many contributions to history include a series of edicts, which were inscribed mostly on pillars and stones.

The Mauryan Empire existed for another fifty-two years after Ashoka's death, but it declined and shrank throughout the reigns of the next six emperors. Maurya was finally overthrown in 185 BCE by Pushyamitra of the Shunga dynasty.

Recognized as an ancient center of learning and culture, particularly during its zenith in the reign of Ashoka, the Mauryan Empire left an indelible mark on history through architecture, edicts, and the unexpected adherence of its first three conquering emperors to non-violent religions while establishing and extending the empire through warfare.

Chapter 1 – Ancient India before Maurya

The Iron Age began in India in 1500 BCE with the spiritual Vedic culture of the northwestern (Punjab) Indo-Aryan people. India began as a subcontinental region that also included parts of the modern-day countries of Pakistan, Bangladesh, and Nepal. Most of the population predominated the Indo-Gangetic Plain—the fertile lands of the Indus and Ganges (Ganga) Rivers that formed the main extent of the occupied Indian subcontinent. As they were bordered by the Himalayas to the north, the Indian population eventually spread down to populate the lands of the Indian Peninsula.

By 326 BCE, the Indian subcontinent was diversified in both language and culture. Hindu rajas ruled small kingdoms or chieftaincies, which were beginning to grow rich in resources and power. This wealth attracted the attention of Alexander the Great, who was poised to invade from the northwest when his troops rebelled, and he subsequently died in 323 BCE. Alexander had spent two years gaining some of the lands of the Punjab region but never accomplished his goal of dominating the Indian subcontinent. Many of Alexander's troops and generals remained within the bounty of the fertile Indus River Valley (forming the western and northwestern boundary of the Indian subcontinent) and laid the foundation for Indo-Greco relations during the Mauryan Empire.

The Vedic religion, also known as ancient Hinduism, was succeeded by Brahmanism (or Brahminism), a form of Hinduism dominated by priestly Brahmans that eventually evolved into contemporary Hinduism. By the sixth century BCE, Hinduism was being eroded by the newly established religions of Jainism and Buddhism. The first three consecutive rulers of the Mauryan Empire adhered to Jainism, Brahmanism, and Buddhism before the empire began reverting to Hinduism. The dissolution of the Mauryan Empire in 185 BCE marked the beginning of the Hindu renaissance, which eventually led to the golden age of the Gupta Empire, which began in the 4th century CE and ended in approximately 550 CE.

Administratively, the Indian subcontinent was governed by a series of chieftaincies, or janapadas. When the Indo-Aryans began migrating south to more fully populate the fertile plains, these chieftaincies began consolidating into kingdoms, also known as the Mahajanapadas. The Mahajanapada of Magadha was situated in the northeastern corner of the populated subcontinent, and its capital, Pataliputra (modern-day Patna in the northeastern state of Bihar), was the setting for the rise and fall of the Maurya Empire.

The existing Nanda Empire of the Magadha region (northeastern subcontinent) controlled the Ganges River trade routes as well as those to the open seaports in the Bay of Bengal. Originating in approximately 345 BCE, the Nanda Empire stretched from Punjab in the west to the Bay of Bengal in the east. It was bordered by the Himalayas to the north and extended south to the Vindhya Range, which means it essentially included the expanse of the fertile Indo-Gangetic Plain. The Nanda Empire grew rich and powerful through trade and the acquisition of natural resources. Their military might was centered in the political capital of Pataliputra.

The Nanda Empire

There were sixteen Mahajanapadas by 325 BCE, and they had all grown rich through the development and trade of iron, as well as through the wise use of other resources or even plunder. Magadha was the most powerful of the four most prominent Mahajanapadas. Its power came from rich iron deposits, which were used to make weaponry or for trade. Magadha also held a strategic position on the northeastern corner of the rich and fertile Indo-Gangetic Plain, where the Indian subcontinent began giving way to modern-day Nepal and Bangladesh. Its capital was protected at the intersection of the Ganges and Son Rivers. Finally, the use of abundant war elephants to dominate in warfare gave Magadha the advantage it needed to get ahead politically.

The Magadhan Empire was the forerunner of the Mauryan dynasties. It is believed the Magadhan Empire started sometime in the 6th century BCE, and it lasted until 321 BCE. The Magadhan Empire has been divided into three great dynasties: the Haryanka dynasty (544– 412 BCE), the Shishunaga dynasty (412– 344 BCE), and finally, the Nanda dynasty (344– 322 BCE). Legends tell that the first great emperor of India, Mahapadma, used a huge army to create the first sole monarchy of the Indian subcontinent, thus beginning the Nanda Empire. After two decades of Nanda rule, Alexander's troops invaded Punjab. At the time, King Dhana Nanda (r. 329– 322 BCE) was on the throne.

The Nanda Empire had been the first in India, and one of the first in the world, to institute a centralized administration from which to govern and draw taxes. Ancient records suggest that the Nanda kings (nine in total) created a currency system and amassed great wealth by dominating trade along the northern reaches of the subcontinent. However, folklore identifies that those in power were also unpopular with their subjects because of their low birth, as well as high taxation and general misconduct and corruption. Legend says that young men across the empire were dissatisfied with the corruption of King Dhana and his Nanda officials, as well as by the excessive use of resources to fight the battles that had established the empire. Along with the fragmentation of the remaining Indian subcontinent into Mahajanapadas and then the eventual death of Alexander the Great, the time was ripe for a power shift and the installation of new leadership.

Historical sources from Iron Age India are convoluted and contradictory, and there is little written history to verify these legends and folktales. Even Greco-Roman sources are confusing and don't lend much weight to Indian accounts. Names and ancestry are particularly confusing; oftentimes, one leader has a surplus of traditional names as well as Greco-Roman names. For these reasons, the history before Maurya, and even the Mauryan dynasty itself, cannot be considered as absolutely accurate or historically factual. Scriptural texts from Hinduism, Buddhism, and Jainism form the basis for indigenous tradition. The Puranas, in particular, are an essential part of ancient Indian literature, and they depict legends and traditional lore. This genre of literature is found in two of the primary religions of India: Hinduism and Jainism. The Puranas were written in Sanskrit, Tamil, and other languages. While the Hindu works are anonymous, the Jain works have attributed authors. The Puranas are very inconsistent and are layered in symbology. The works cannot always be considered as direct facts but sometimes rather allegories for the truth; they are also not technically scriptures but rather remembrances of culture. There are thirty-six major and minor Puranas, which contain over 400,000 verses. Thought to be written between the 3rd and 10th century CE, the Puranas were supposed to have served an encyclopedic function in their time, as they include detailed information on geography, history, politics, astronomy, creation theories, cosmology, and philosophy (as well as a list of the Mauryan kings). Works such as the play *Mudrarakshasa*, "The Ring of Rakshasa" (a drama written by Vishakhadatta that is set in the 4th and 3rd century BCE), and the Kashmiri *Kathasaritsagara* (a collection of folktale stories by the Shaivite Somadeva, written in the 11th century

CE) are also critically important sources of history. Other religious works, such as the Jain *Parishishtaparvan*, which was composed by a 12th-century Jain writer named Hemachandra, and many other texts across the Buddhist, Hindu, and Jain belief systems have supplied legendary references that enable the Mauryan story to be pieced together, if not factually then at least metaphorically. Along with archaeological findings and Greco-Roman references, the apocryphal evidence can, at times, be substantiated or at least provide a more detailed picture of possibilities.

What is clear, however, is that the center of power was the capital of Pataliputra in Magadha (modern-day Patna). The Nandas mostly controlled the capital province and the Ganges valleys that ran west and northwest toward the Indus Valley, which separates modern-day India from Pakistan. In 326 BCE, Alexander's army was poised at the western perimeters to invade the Nanda territories, but the armies did not get a chance to meet in battle. The Macedonian troops refused to go any farther when they discovered the extent and resources of the Nanda army. King Dhana Nanda (known to the Greco-Roman world as Xandrames or Agrammes) was said to have controlled an immense and terrifying army of 20,000 cavalry, 200,000 infantry, 2,000 chariots, and 3,000 elephants, as well as vast monetary resources. The demoralized Macedonian army mutinied, forcing Alexander to withdraw and ultimately return to Babylon (Iraq), where he died in 323 BCE.

According to folklore, the Nanda Empire's capital was also a place of learning, culture, and art. Economically, the Nanda dynasty was strong, and they began a system of common coinage, which continued into the Mauryan dynasty. It is not clear whether the Nanda kings had exclusive access to iron ore mines or other rich mineral deposits or whether they controlled other resources like timber and elephants, but many historical sources refer to the great wealth of the Nanda Empire. There were even rumors of the last Nanda king hoarding great treasure in the Ganges riverbed, only for it to be swept away in the floods and deposited on the alluvial plains!

Overtaxation and greed became the downfall of the Nanda Empire, along with the general opinion that the rulers were of low birth and not righteous in their conduct. Both this civil fragmentation and the aborted invasion by Alexander formed the ideal conditions for a change in power. Ancient indigenous sources tell of the rise of the strategic and ambitious Chanakya (c. 350– 275 BCE), who, for some reason, had been present at the Nanda royal court, possibly as a royal advisor, but had been insulted and left. In revenge, Chanakya proceeded to instigate an uprising to overthrow the Nanda dynasty.

[1] An artist's impression of Chanakya (possibly also known as Kautilya or Vishnugupta). Chanakya is historically attributed with putting the first ruler of the Mauryan Empire, Chandragupta Maurya, in power.

Most sources broadly agree that Chanakya was a scholar from Takshashila (modern-day Taxila, Pakistan). He was well versed in several of the Hindi Vedas (scriptural texts) and also had a good understanding of politics and economics. He was a Brahmin—a Hindu priest—who was focused on teaching and passing on sacred learning across generations. Brahmins were not necessarily simply holy men. They held the highest status in Hindu society and could also be farmers, soldiers, or tradespeople. In Chanakya's case, he was a professor specializing in religion, mathematics, science, geography, and later politics.

It is likely that Chanakya was present in Taxila when Alexander's troops invaded Punjab. Chanakya saw the Greek influence as a potential threat to the Indian culture and began seeking inroads with King Dhana Nanda. Of the many confusing sources regarding Chanakya, one of the common threads is that during a visit to the capital of the Nanda kings—Pataliputra—he was insulted and left in a rage, vowing to bring down the empire. Other sources claim that Chanakya was more involved in the Nanda dynasty at the capital and that he was a minister of the court. He argued with King Dhana Nanda and either left in a rage or fled for his life westward toward Ujjain or Ujjaini (the western extremities of the greater Magadha region) or north to Taxila. He set out to find somebody worthy of his assistance in gaining power and overthrowing the Nanda dynasty. We will never know how much of this tale is true, although we do know that Chanakya and the future founder of the Maurya Empire—Chandragupta Maurya—were consorts. Chanakya already had allies from his association with Taxila, such as the Punjab rulers and the Himalayan King Parvata (Porus), and together with Chandragupta, they began gathering forces and resources for a rebellion.

Chapter 2 – Rise of the Mauryan Empire

The Installment of Chandragupta Maurya

The Mauryan story begins with the relatively obscure figure of Chandragupta Maurya (c. 340– 297 BCE), who attracted the attention of the politically well-positioned but disgruntled Chanakya. (There are many Chandraguptas throughout Indian history, which is why the addition of Maurya is used. Chandragupta was known as Sandrokottos or Androcottus to the Western world at the time.) Legend tells that Chanakya had been grievously insulted by King Dhana Nanda and vowed revenge and the complete destruction of the Nanda Empire. As a mentor to Chandragupta Maurya, Chanakya used his considerable persuasive power, intelligence network, and other resources to wage a series of battles that eventually put Chandragupta in power, with Chanakya as his chief advisor.

[2] Statue of Chandragupta Maurya (r. 321–297 BCE), founder of the Mauryan Empire: Laxminarayan Temple, New Delhi, India.

Chanakya had been a scholar of Taxila, a strategically located urban node in Punjab where the Indian subcontinent met central Asia. Chanakya, also known as Kautilya or Vishnugupta, was possibly politically involved in the Nanda Empire when he was purportedly offended by King Dhana Nanda. Chanakya left the capital of Pataliputra in Magadha, after which he met Chandragupta as a boy or young man. He took Chandragupta under his tutelage, with a long-term vision of using him to eliminate the Nanda Empire. It is not clear why he chose to incite Chandragupta specifically to create a rebellion against the Nanda Empire except that his young charge may have displayed more than ordinary intelligence and skills.

Much of the history of the Mauryan Empire can be attributed to two ancient works, as well as the edicts of Ashoka, the third Mauryan emperor. One of these ancient works was a treatise, the *Arthashastra*, which was allegedly authored by Chanakya. It describes the statecraft, economic policy, and military strategy of the time in ancient Indian Sanskrit. The second well-known source is a play called *Mudrarakshasa* by the Indian Sanskrit poet and playwright Vishakhadatta. However, neither the *Arthashastra* nor the *Mudrarakshasa* has managed to paint a clear picture of Chanakya and his accomplice Chandragupta Maurya, so the real details of Chandragupta's meteoric rise to power remain largely a mystery.

But who was Chandragupta, and why was he chosen by Chanakya to be the political figurehead? It is widely accepted that it was Chanakya, not Chandragupta Maurya, who engineered the dismantling of the Nanda dynasty and the establishment of the Mauryan Empire in 321 BCE (also recorded as 322 BCE in some sources). Chanakya took the young Chandragupta under his wing, and together, they established a strategic hold on the Mauryan Empire, first through warfare and then via political maneuvering and murder.

Some records describe the interrelationship between Chandragupta Maurya and Chanakya as so intertwined that they could be confused as the same person. There is evidence that Chandragupta Maurya was a descendant of the royal Nanda Empire, but other evidence points to him being of lowly birth and that his special skills and intelligence attracted the attention of the learned and politically sophisticated Chanakya. One particular source describes Chandragupta Maurya as the grandson of Nanda King Sarvartha-siddhi. Other records claim that as a young and unknown soldier of a low caste, he led a campaign to expel the Greek invaders. Certain histories position Chandragupta as a military man who sought to play a role in Alexander's campaigns, and once he was rejected, he learned military skills from the Nanda army and then from Chanakya. Several Greco-Roman historians, including Plutarch (c. 46- 120 CE) and

Megasthenes (c. 350–290 BCE), the latter of whom attended the Mauryan royal court, mention a meeting between Alexander and Chandragupta that ended in disaster. What is most likely, however, is that no matter Chandragupta's lineage or career path, he was of a similar caste (social class) to Chanakya. They probably belonged to Kshatriya (ruler/warrior caste), which would have been one of the most likely reasons to bring them into contact.

Most histories suggest a long and intimate association between Chandragupta and Chanakya, in which Chanakya was a mentor, teacher, and influencer. It is evident that Chanakya's aim was a centralized pan-Indian empire that could restore order and fend off invaders. The fragmented republics and kingdoms were clearly not able to create peace or adequately protect the borders of the subcontinental kingdoms. It is also clear that Chandragupta and Chanakya took advantage of the political turmoil created by the departure of Alexander's troops and amassed resources and political allies to support their cause of overthrowing the Nanda dynasty. Buddhist legends suggest that the Nanda monarchy was strong at its core in Pataliputra but that their influence weakened farther from the capital. Apparently, after an initial aborted attempt at taking the capital, Chandragupta leveraged this situation by conquering outlying areas of the realm before turning his attention on the capital. Some of the outlying areas taken by Chandragupta Maurya were the regions previously conquered by Alexander the Great. It is likely that he used this recaptured northwestern territory as a base from which to capture Magadha. Most sources describe a long preparatory period in which Chandragupta Maurya was tutored by Chanakya in statecraft and warfare, during which Chandragupta also learned to be a soldier, although it is entirely possible that he could have been a part of the Nanda army or even under Alexander the Great during his conquest years in the northwest. What is clear is that Chandragupta began gaining power and ground in the northwestern territories where the Nanda hold was weakest.

Death and Deception to Gain and Retain Power

Irrespective of who really held power or intent in the Chanakya and Chandragupta Maurya relationship, they began their conquest of the Nanda Empire through the formation of an alliance with the powerful King Parvata (or Porus), whose realm lay along the northwestern Himalayan boundary. Folklore suggests that Chandragupta and Chanakya were well connected politically and socially and began their alliances through not only the recruitment of King Parvata and his son, Malayaketu, but also with the governor of Taxila, several of Chanakya's students, and other eminent persons in powerful and influential positions, such as the rulers of small subcontinental Indian states. Chanakya used his extensive intelligence network and considerable powers of persuasion to gather up men and resources from across the greater Magadha region and other provinces—men who were apparently disgruntled with the Nanda rulership of corruption and oppression. It is even highly probable that many of their soldiers would have been unemployed Greek troops (*Yona* or *Yavana*) taken on as paid mercenaries.

Chandragupta's army began gaining inroads into the Nanda Empire by attacking and dominating the outer villages of the Nanda frontiers. Accumulating support and resources as they went, they established garrisons in their conquered lands and gained allies who were keen to overthrow the unpopular Nandas. (The unpopularity of the Nanda kings was confirmed in Plutarch's *Life of Alexander*.) After an apparent initial defeat to capture Pataliputra, they agreed to create an allied army with many more powerful fiefdoms. Buddhist legends suggest that the final militia that overthrew the Nanda dynasty consisted of Macedonians (*Yavanas*), Himalayans (Kiratas), Scythians (Shakas), Kambojas, Persians (*Parasikas*), and the Bactrians (Bahlikas).

With the intent to divide and conquer, this allied army launched a series of battles, eventually invading Pataliputra (also known as Kusumapura, "City of Flowers"), this time successfully. Legend states that they met the Nanda general, Bhadrasala, outside of the city walls and laid siege to the capital. It was within this atmosphere of civil unrest that the heir to the Nanda kingdom was assassinated. King Dhana escaped into exile, leaving his prime minister, Rakshasa, behind—or at least so the folktales state. It is also possible that King Dhana Nanda died in the battle. Some sources suggest that the final overthrow of Magadha was extremely difficult and that Chandragupta Maurya and Chanakya employed mercenaries to attack the ruling army and executed guerilla tactics because the Nanda army was too powerful to take head-on.

By the time Chandragupta Maurya ascended the throne, he was about twenty-five years old. The allied forces took time to consolidate the capital in the midst of animosity and danger. Chandragupta narrowly escaped an assassination attempt at the beginning of his reign from a girl who had been sent by Rakshasa, the escaped former prime minister of the Nanda Empire. Chanakya intercepted the assassin and instead redirected the killer to their ally, King Parvata, casting the blame of Parvata's death on Rakshasa. Parvata's son, Malayaketu, uncovered the deception and allied himself with the exiled Rakshasa. More assassination attempts were made by Rakshasa, but they were all foiled by the ever-watchful Chanakya.

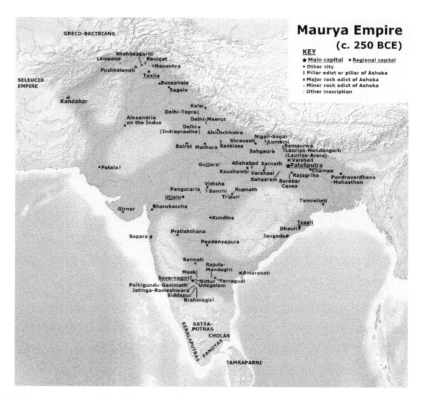

[3] The extent of the Mauryan Empire during the reign of Chandragupta's grandson, Ashoka, in 250 BCE gives an idea of the potential extremities of the empire. Chandragupta managed to recapture the northwestern territories and came to dominate most of the northern Indo-Gangetic Plain. It is unlikely that his realm ever stretched farther south than Karnataka. The eastern territory (in green) shows the illusive Kalinga region and the location of the Dhauli edict (likely location of the Kalinga War).

Chanakya, the real power behind the newly installed Mauryan throne, continued to plot, lie, and murder, ensuring that the stronghold of Chandragupta Maurya remained intact. He turned allies against each other and royal brothers against brothers until Rakshasa and Malayaketu formed an alliance of five kings, which included soldiers from seven farther-away territories. A covert war of spying and deception ensued, orchestrated by the meddling Chanakya. Chanakya finally achieved his ends when the main enemy of the Mauryan Empire, Malayaketu, was tricked into destroying his primary allies and was subsequently deserted by his remaining allies. Ultimately, Rakshasa returned to become Chandragupta Maurya's prime minister through Chanakya's trickery. He pledged allegiance to the Mauryan emperor, requesting a pardon for Malayaketu. Although it is impossible to confirm how much of this covert war is true, the contents of the *Arthashastra* point specifically to spying, assassination, and other elements of an ancient secret service as strategies to gain and retain power. The Mauryan rulers did not dismiss political subterfuge or even torture as outside of their prerogative.

Chanakya's work in installing the new Indian rulership was complete. Whether fiend or visionary, the royal advisor's role in history has been heralded as a watershed moment, as it united the Indian subcontinent and laid the groundwork for powerful economic strategies and international diplomacy, not to mention the birth of an expansive place of learning and culture. Although historically labeled as a scheming alchemist and master manipulator, he has also been attributed (at least in part) with the creation of the *Arthashastra* ("The Science of Material Gain"), a critically valuable treatise on socio-economics, politics, and governance that miraculously survived the ages. The *Arthashastra* is a valuable source of history and ancient culture, and its policies for economic development and statecraft are still relevant today. Along with the *Arthashastra*, the *Chanakya Niti*, a compendium of aphorisms, is another work attributed to Chanakya. Whether Chanakya held an altruistic and united vision for India or whether he was a self-interested and power-hungry oligarch (or perhaps something in between), he is viewed favorably in today's political world as a powerful thinker, philosopher, and diplomat who made significant headway in bringing the Indian subcontinent under a single rule. Chanakya states in his *Arthashastra* that it was the Nanda kings who engaged in duplicity, intrigue, and poor dharma (incorrect action) in the kingdom, which was restored by Chandragupta Maurya, who ruled with love, tolerance, and virtuosity and who was loved by his subjects. Although this statement is more than likely heavily biased, it shows his aptitude for spinning things so Chandragupta and the Maurya Empire came out on top.

Chanakya continued as a chief advisor (and possibly later as prime minister) to Chandragupta at the royal center of Pataliputra and then to his son, Bindusara. Legends say that before the end of his life, Chanakya left the royal court to die alone in isolation, leaving the *Arthashastra* behind. This historical treatise documented the requirements of a ruler to remain in power. While strategy, governance, and economics were discussed, spying, subterfuge, and assassination were described in equal measure. The creation of the Mauryan dynasty may have been part of a broader continental vision by its founders, but historians continue to ask the age-old question: Did the ends justify the means?

The origin of the name "Maurya" is not entirely clear. The most likely source of the name is from the Moriya clan of the Shakyas (greater Magadha culture) to which Chandragupta belonged. The Buddha came from the noble Shakya clan, and they were considered the seed stock of both Buddhism and Jainism. Although many sources refer to the dynasty as Maurya, neither Ashoka's edicts nor contemporary Greek accounts use this name. There is also a possible connection to peacocks, which has been an ongoing symbol of Indian dynasties and currently India's national bird. Chandragupta Maurya is potentially thought to have been the son of the royal superintendent of peacocks (*mayura-poshaka*). The connection between peacocks and the place of the Mauryan kings (Magadha) continues through Buddhist tradition, which states that their ancestors settled "in the place of peacocks" and potentially built a city named *Moriya-nagara* using peacock-colored bricks. The word peacock is *mora* in Pali, an ancient local Magadha language, and *mayura* in Sanskrit. Regardless of whether the peacock was the source for the name Maurya or not, the peacock remained an important Mauryan symbol and appeared on architecture, such as the pillars of Ashoka and at the Buddhist center of Sanchi. It is likely that the peacock was the dynasty's emblem. Although Ashoka's inscriptions and the contemporary Greek accounts do not mention the name Maurya, it does appear on other Indian rock inscriptions from various time periods, such as the Junagadh rock inscription of Rudradaman from 150 CE and the Kuntala inscription from the 12th century CE. The name is also mentioned as a dynasty in various texts, for example, the Puranas and Buddhist, Jain, and Tamil literature.

Even though the specifics of Chandragupta Maurya's rise to power remain obscure, once the capital was stabilized, the newly installed Mauryan monarchy slowly but surely began gaining provinces. Almost two decades into his reign, the Mauryan Empire included a large swathe of land that stretched from modern-day Afghanistan in the west (including the Hindu-Kush) to the Bay of Bengal in the east. It extended south to include the fertile lands of the Indo-Gangetic Plain and most of the northern section of the Indian subcontinent except the main peninsula. Maurya was a single state governed from within and was establishing itself as an ancient superpower.

Chapter 3 – The Greco-Roman Affiliation

Once in power, Chandragupta Maurya continued his expansion of the empire and brought the northwestern territories under subjugation. Magadha had been more easily settled into its own kingdom for many generations, where smaller principalities had amalgamated into the relatively protected capital province. It was the northwestern extremities of the realm that had been more exposed. The Himalayas formed a boundary to the north with the Arabian Sea to the west, but the passes through the Hindu Kush (such as the Khyber Pass between Afghanistan and Pakistan) made Punjab vulnerable. Before the creation of the Mauryan Empire, Alexander marched his troops toward the Indian subcontinent. He was intent on "world" conquest. The rulers of Taxila and Abhisara surrendered, but King Parvata (Porus) of Punjab refused to do the same. During the Battle of the Hydaspes, on the banks of the river Jhelum, Porus was defeated but treated respectfully by Alexander. However, Alexander's forces refused to go any farther. Exhausted from warfare, having been absent from home for many years, and informed of the military might of Magadha, they mutinied. Alexander accepted temporary defeat and returned home to Babylon, where he unexpectedly died at the age of thirty-three, never to complete his dreamed-of domination of India.

During his retreat, Alexander had made the necessary administrative arrangements for his conquered lands along the way.

Before his death, the Macedonian conqueror had left Seleucus I Nicator as his satrap (provincial governor or prefect) in charge of the northwestern territories that bordered the Magadhan lands. Alexander died shortly before the creation of the Maurya Empire, but Macedonian legions remained at the outposts of their conquered lands in a similar manner to the post-Roman Byzantine Empire. The vast area of what became the Seleucid Empire stretched from the borders of the Indian subcontinent in the east to include most of modern-day Turkey, Iran, Kuwait, Afghanistan, and Turkmenistan, as well as ancient Mesopotamia and the Levant.

The Persian provinces within modern-day Afghanistan, as well as the wealthy Kingdom of Gandhara and the Indus Valley states, had all submitted to Alexander before his death. Successive power struggles within the Macedonian leadership had left Seleucus I Nicator (358–281 BCE) in control of what became the Seleucid Empire. The Seleucid Empire included Persia (Iran) and Bactria by 312 BCE. Seleucid went on to become the second most expansive empire in western Asia, rivaled only by the extent of Alexander's territory at the height of his domination. However, the easternmost reaches of the Seleucid Empire always remained in the Indus River Valley because of the Mauryan presence.

In 317 BCE, Chandragupta Maurya reverted his attention back to the Punjab area, specifically the occupied territories under the control of Seleucus I Nicator. By 316 BCE, Chandragupta laid claim to the whole of the northwestern subcontinent and had regained the Macedonian satraps taken by Alexander the Great up to the Indus River. Seleucus crossed the Indus to defend any further shrinkage of his territories in 305 BCE. However, after two years of cross-boundary skirmishes, which is known as the Seleucid-Mauryan War, the Treaty of the Indus was ratified with Chandragupta Maurya as the victor.

History does not suggest that the Seleucid-Mauryan War was a single pitched battle, and it is also likely that Seleucus I Nicator, like the Macedonian troops of Alexander's day, was reluctant to make a full onslaught against the might of the Indian subcontinent. Histories suggest that Chandragupta was always intent on taking back the northwestern territories lost during Alexander's time and that several Greek governors were killed when the Mauryan armies freed Indian land from the Macedonians.

Chandragupta not only took back the lands east of the Indus River but also further intimidated the enemy into relinquishing more territory. Fearing further invasion into his empire, Seleucus I Nicator was forced to submit to Chandragupta Maurya and eventually ceded an enormous tract of land west of the Indus, as well as a Macedonian princess in marriage, who may have been his daughter. Another version of the Treaty of the Indus states that it was the agreement that Macedonians and Indians could intermarry rather than the offering of a Macedonian princess.

The Mauryan hegemony had triumphed using the largest army of their time, which included legendary numbers of more than half a million men (foot soldiers), 30,000 cavalry, and 9,000 war elephants. Chandragupta sealed the alliance by gifting 500 war elephants and other supplies. In return, Chandragupta acquired portions of land known today as Afghanistan (the Hindu Kush) and the Balochistan province of Pakistan. These war elephants were instrumental in the expansion of the Seleucid Empire in the west and north, as well as in Seleucus's decisive fight of the Diadochi (conflicts fought between Alexander's successors), the Battle of Ipsus.

During an era of campaigning and territorial domination, this diplomatic exchange was a brilliant move to establish and maintain peaceful Indo-Greco relations for generations to come. The Seleucid Empire lasted until 63 BCE—over a century longer than the Mauryan Empire. The Treaty of the Indus allowed the Mauryan Empire to expand south and east with the knowledge that the exposed northwestern border had been secured with a lasting arrangement. The friendly relations established with the treaty lasted not only throughout Chandragupta's reign but also throughout the 140-year existence of the Mauryan Empire. There are even classical records that suggest that Chandragupta Maurya sent potions and gifts to Seleucus I Nicator, including aphrodisiacs!

Most importantly, the two leaders established an early form of international relations with the Seleucid ambassador Megasthenes (c. 350– 290 BCE). This Greek ambassador was responsible for writing a book named *Indika* and was posted to the Mauryan court for four years. Megasthenes had been born in Asia Minor (modern-day Turkey) and was an ethnographer and diplomat.

Unfortunately, *Indika* in its entirety has been lost, but some of its contents have been made available through references by other ancient Greco-Roman historians and biographers, who occasionally directly paraphrase *Indika's* original content. *Indika* provides insight into the Mauryan Empire, in which Megasthenes describes Pataliputra as one of the first urban nodes (cities) in the world to have a highly efficient form of local self-government. He stated that Chandragupta's rule was marked by three parallel administrative systems. The first was overseeing the villages (rural life), including all aspects of the land and resources. The second arm managed city affairs, mostly involving trade and industry. The third section of the government concerned itself with the military and warfare.

Megasthenes goes on to describe a city fifteen by two kilometers in dimension protected by an immense timber palisade boasting 570 towers and 64 gates. Other evidence of official buildings at that time suggest influences borrowed from Persia and Macedonia. There is evidence of a pillared hypostyle hall in the capital adorned with gold and silver leaf and reports that Chandragupta wore fine embroidered muslins. Later, in Ashoka's time, sandstone often replaced the wood, upon which intricate designs were carved. *Indika* was also instrumental in describing ancient Indian gods, religions, and the geographical features of the Indian subcontinent and the Himalayas.

In approximately 292 BCE, Seleucus appointed his son Antiochos I as viceroy to the eastern provinces of the Seleucid Empire. Antiochos sent the Seleucid diplomat Deimakos to Bindusara's (Chandragupta's son and successor) court in a similar manner as Megasthenes had been sent to Chandragupta's court. Deimakos (also spelled as Deimachus) wrote extensively on the Indian subcontinent, as well as the Mauryan Empire, although his writings have been lost. The friendly relations with the Greek empires beyond Maurya's borders meant that the Khyber Pass, which links modern-day Afghanistan to Pakistan, was no longer considered a weak point. The pass now formed an important passage through which international trade in goods and culture could now move; in fact, it was encouraged.

Although Maurya existed before the Roman Empire (which began in 27 BCE), during Rome's 500 year-long domination of western Asia, many writers and philosophers traveled through its dominions, recording present and past history. These include such famous persons as Plutarch (c. 46- 120 CE), Pliny the Elder (c. 23- 79 CE), and Arrian (c. 86- 160 CE). These post-dynastic writings have served as valuable sources of information and ideas regarding the Maurya Empire. In terms of India as a whole, the three most significant texts providing insight into ancient cultures are Strabo's (Greco-Roman, c. 64 BCE- 21 CE) *Geography*, Ptolemy's (Greco-Egyptian, 2nd century CE) *A Guide to Geography*, and a text called *Periplus of the Erythrean Sea* (a Greco-Roman travel book written in the 1st century CE). These combined surviving texts collectively describe thriving port cities, great urban nodes, and prosperous trade. Many texts refer to the mineral wealth of India, which would have included diamonds, pearls, and semi-precious stones. (Mining was clearly prevalent, and the extracted metals formed the basis for weaponry and other tools.) It seems that the Indians likewise sent representatives to Greek and Roman cities, mainly philosophers and sages, to share wisdom, knowledge, and learning. It was evident that the Indian culture was respected and revered but not entirely accepted, as the Indians had practices such as burning widows and the unfair caste system, which prevented organic movement of people through social classes and even intermarriage.

The Roman historian Justin, who wrote on the kings of Macedonia, had some fascinating things to say about Chandragupta Maurya, which was obviously not firsthand information. It is hard to say when Justin lived, but it was certainly not during the existence of the Maurya Empire. Scholars place his works as being written anywhere between the 2nd century and 3rd century.

Justin XV.4.12-13 and 19:

> India, after the death of Alexander, had assassinated his prefects [governors], as if shaking the burden of servitude. The author of this liberation was Sandracottos [Chandragupta Maurya], but he had transformed liberation in servitude after victory, since, after taking the throne, he himself oppressed the very people he has liberated from domination.

> Later, as he [Chandragupta] was preparing war against the prefects of Alexander, a huge wild elephant went to him and took him on his back as if tame, and he became a remarkable fighter and war leader. Having thus acquired royal power, Sandracottos possessed India at the time Seleucos was preparing future glory.

Once Chandragupta Maurya had established peace along the northwestern border of his lands, he turned his attention to capturing control of the east (except Kalinga) and the south (the Deccan Plateau). By the end of his reign, Chandragupta Maurya controlled the entirety of the northern length of the Indian subcontinent. Known to the Greek world as Sandrokottos (or Androcottus), Chandragupta Maurya created a royal court that became a bustling metropolis of learning and culture and provided the fertile environment from which Chanakya's famous political-economic treatise, the *Arthashastra*, was born. Maurya's capital, Pataliputra, was administered by six committees with five members apiece. The emperor had a council of ministers (*amatya*), with Chanakya as his chief minister. Chandragupta set up and managed a strong central government and held power by dividing his dominion into manageable provinces, with each being overseen by a reigning prince. The central government maintained a further two dozen departments that were responsible for various social and economic responsibilities, such as aspects of trade, the marketing of goods, medical care and sanitation, demographic records, and foreign relations. This geopolitical arrangement continued to be effective in the reigns of his descendants and beyond.

Chandragupta was very involved in all matters of state and warfare, even relying on a network of spies to achieve his ends and, if it was called for, resorting to torture. In a pervasive era of suspicion and control, the first ruler of the Mauryan Empire had control over a huge army of troops (*maula*), which were all recruited, trained, and equipped by the state. *Atavika* (forest tribes) paid mercenaries (*bhrita*), and corporate guilds of soldiers (*shreni*) added to Maurya's military might. It has been recorded that Greek troops (*Yavanas*) assisted Chandragupta Maurya, particularly during the initial conquest of the Nanda dynasty. There were four sections (*chaturanga*) to the Mauryan army: infantry, cavalry (with catapults), chariots, and elephants. The war office of the central government employed thirty people to command the Mauryan army, as well as to see over aspects of the newly formed navy and other land transportation. The Roman writer Pliny estimated Chandragupta's army included 600,000 infantry, 30,000 cavalry, 8,000 chariots, and 9,000 elephants. Mauryan warfare was described as being organized into formations (*vyuhas*) to suit the terrain and enemy. Great lengths were taken to train men and animals in the art of war, and both the emperors and princes were expected to be trained and to participate in battles. The Mauryan navy was mentioned little in the *Arthashastra*, but it is believed they were deployed to protect the coastlines and along the riverways to support the trade networks.

It was the Mauryan army that was all important. Soldiers were either scantily clad or wore quilted cotton shirts. They fought with bows and arrows, swords, and double-handed broadswords, shields (mostly made of hides), javelins, lances, axes, pikes, clubs, and maces. Thickly coiled turbans adorned their heads, as well as bands of cloth around their middles or chests for protection. Sometimes they wore tunics in winter or the drawer style kilt, tucked between the legs. The Mauryan's gargantuan army was funded by the vast resources and trade routes that they controlled, as well as by taxes raised from their expanding dominions. No matter the shady beginnings of Chandragupta Maurya's reign, there can be no doubt that the empire he handed to his son, Bindusara, had grown to mythical and all-powerful proportions. Unfortunately, Chandragupta's era of suspicion and control continued for over half a century, lasting into the reign of his grandson, Ashoka.

The Mauryan Empire was characterized by nine main rulers, with the first three being the longest and most powerful. After the conversion of the most determined of the Mauryan rulers (Ashoka) to the peaceful ways of Buddhism, the empire began to weaken and disband. History suggests that espionage and bloody warfare may have been the only methods to successfully achieve and maintain national unity. However, the Mauryan Empire remains a paradox since all its emperors practiced religious and spiritual tolerance as well as patronized culture and the arts. They were also instrumental in the development of religious buildings, shrines, and other architecture. Maurya's 136-year domination of the subcontinent was considered a stable time of economic prosperity and socioeconomic reforms and of the development of infrastructure and assistance for marginalized communities. The crime rate was low, and pomp and pageantry were prevalent, as there were many celebrations and festivals.

A unified empire came at a cost to its founding emperor, Chandragupta, who constantly thought that he would be assassinated. He took extreme measures to ensure he remained unharmed, using a prodigious network of spies to keep him informed of the activities in his provincial kingdoms and eventually turning to religion and spirituality to alleviate the pressures of a twenty-four year-long rule. Chandragupta finally turned to Jainism to provide himself with spiritual succor. Both Buddhism and Jainism are associated with non-violence (including vegetarianism), asceticism, and traditions that require adherence to strict codes of behavior and morals devoid of "sin." Jainism was a peaceful religion that amalgamated the established Hindu traditions with elements of the increasing influence of Buddhism, and it remains prevalent in India today. By the end of his life, Chandragupta eventually gave up rulership completely and lived as a Jain monk. He ultimately starved himself to death in 297 BCE as part of his religious tradition. There is confusion over whether he died in office or abdicated to his son, Bindusara. It seems more likely that he would have, at least in part, abdicated because of his deep association with the ascetic life at the end of his reign. Chandragupta is rumored to have traveled south to Karnataka on a pilgrimage to commit the Jain ritual of *sallekhana* (fasting to death).

Chapter 4 – Growth of the Empire

The Mauryan Empire continued with Chandragupta's son, Bindusara (r. c. 297– 273 BCE), who supposedly ascended the throne at just twenty-two years of age. Virtually nothing is known about the personal lives of the Mauryan kings except that it was an ancestral dynasty, meaning the nine rulers were all sons of their fathers or at least their next of kin. Bindusara was also known by the Sanskrit name of Amitraghata ("Slayer of Enemies") and the Greek name of Amitrochates. Like his father before him and his son—Ashoka—who succeeded him, Bindusara ruled for a very long time, approximately a quarter of a century. Bindusara is the least well known of the first three mighty Mauryan kings. His obscurity is most likely because he was not a stalwart advocate of either Jainism (like his father, Chandragupta) or of Buddhism (like his son, Ashoka); therefore, very few scriptural texts about his reign exist.

Bindusara is best remembered as the emperor who came between the two most well-known emperors. There are some Buddhist, Jain, and Hindu traditional accounts, as well as Greek references, to him. Evidence suggests that Bindusara was an intellectual with cosmopolitan tastes. Buddhist traditions describe Bindusara as the conqueror that significantly extended the Mauryan Empire by gaining the southern lands to include the extremities that his son Ashoka inherited—the Deccan Plateau between the Western and Eastern Ghats mountain ranges up to Karnataka. Some legends say that Bindusara captured sixteen new territories and was the ruler of the "land between two seas"—meaning the entire Indian Peninsula between the Arabian Sea and the Bay of Bengal. Bindusara also held the rest of the Indian subcontinent northwards as well as parts of Afghanistan and Balochistan (Pakistan). However, other accounts suggest Bindusara did not gain new lands but rather managed to hold what he had acquired from his father's reign by eliminating petty squabbles and uprisings. Whatever territorial gains Bindusara managed to make, he is definitely attributed with the consolidation and organization of the empire, thus continuing and building on his father's social and economic work.

Some scholars believe the mentions of Bindusara taking the Deccan Plateau is talking about the suppression of revolts and not the conquering of new land. The folklore of the southern kingdom of the Tamils (natives of the southernmost Tamil Nadu state) speaks of them repulsing Mauryan might, which was true for the duration of the Mauryan reign. The very southern peninsula of the Indian subcontinent remained independent, as the Tamils continued their dominance there, but the pillars of Ashoka clarify that the Tamils remained on friendly terms with the Maurya Empire. Although none of the Mauryan emperors managed to conquer the Tamil state at the southern tip of India, ancient Tamil literature, such as Sangam literature (apocryphal writings dating from 300 BCE), suggests that southern India was invaded by Mauryan troops at certain times. Some verses describe Mauryan troops from Karnataka invading areas south of the Deccan Plateau. Other writings, including Greek sources, confirm such an invasion, although it seems that the Mauryans were defeated, and Tamil Nadu retained its independence under King Ilamchetchenni of the Cholas. The Tamil country, along with the Pandyas and the Cheras, was generally considered to be friendly in Mauryan times.

Another area eluded both Chandragupta and Bindusara—parts of modern-day northern Andhra Pradesh and its northeastern neighbor, Odisha, both on the eastern edge of the Maurya Empire. Collectively known by the ancient Indian name of Kalinga, this forested area was home to a powerful, independent tribe known as the Kalingas, who had also evaded rule by the Nandas. Kalinga was a large central-eastern fertile area stretching from the Bay of Bengal in the east and including approximately the territories of modern-day Odisha and some of northeastern Andhra Pradesh, as well as northern Telangana and some of Madhya Pradesh. Although the extent of Kalinga changed over time, the borders were the Godavari River to the south and the Mahanadi River to the north, with the western border shifting according to conquests over time but generally reaching as far into the hinterland as central India. Rich in natural resources, metals, and minerals, and with access to the sea, Kalinga remained independent into the rule of Ashoka. Kalinga was prosperous and strategically placed, as it was close to the capital in the north at Magadha and had good access to trade routes to eastern Asia.

Most accounts state that Chanakya was still an important part of the Mauryan court during Bindusara's reign and that Chanakya's treatise, the *Arthashastra*, continued to be a reference for statecraft into Ashoka's reign. Chanakya was thought to have continued in the role of prime minister at least during part of Bindusara's rule, and medieval writings recorded that he assisted Bindusara in conquering new lands, just as he had done for his father, Chandragupta Maurya. Several legends suggest that the northwestern territory of Taxila revolted twice during Bindusara's reign. His eldest son and heir to the throne, Susima (Sushima), was accused of maladministration in the first instance, and it was only during Ashoka's reign that the uprisings in Taxila were finally quelled.

There are legends that Bindusara had hundreds of councilors, two of which—Khallataka and Radhagupta—assisted in putting Ashoka on the throne after his death. During the height of the Mauryan Empire, there were twenty-seven superintendents (*adhyakshas*) who were responsible for economic activities from agriculture and mining to weaving and spinning. Irrigation facilities and reservoirs were a priority for agriculture, and the infrastructure for these was commissioned and overseen by the state. The standardization of weights and measures for trade and all other parts of the empire's economy was prevalent during the Mauryan Empire. This enabled the administration to keep careful records of the national accounting system, particularly for the purposes of taxation. Taxes were gathered from all corners of the realm and from all strata of the social classes. State resources were not only taxed in coin but also in kind, and a great deal of time was given to the actual assessment of tax collection.

Megasthenes mentioned seven castes of the population: philosophers, soldiers, Brahmins (priests), craftsmen, herdsmen, farmers, and magistrates. This social arrangement seemed to be according to occupation rather than birth, although it is well known that a caste system based upon one's social class at birth was prevalent before and after the Maurya Empire. Although polygamy was practiced amongst the upper classes, the Hindu concept of Stridhana interestingly applied to women. Stridhana enabled women to work for their money and to retain their own wealth if they separated from their husbands—this specifically included marriage gifts. Megasthenes also noted that enforced slavery was not apparent in the subcontinent but that there were servants.

Bindusara continued good diplomatic relations with the Greek world and possibly extended his international connections as far as Egypt. As mentioned above, Seleucid I Nicator's son, Antiochos I, sent his ambassador, Deimakos (or Deimachus) of Plateia, to the Mauryan court. There is further evidence of Greek authors being welcomed in Bindusara's court (such as Iambulus), as well as a request made to Antiochos for a sophist (a classical Greek teacher), which was refused because they were not for sale. Deimakos was responsible for the creation of the treatise "On Piety" (*Peri Eusebeias*) and is known to have written extensively on India, although, sadly, these texts are lost. Like the other key figures of the Mauryan Empire, Bindusara enjoyed learning and foreign civilizations, and he maintained Hellenic international relations not just politically but also socio-culturally.

The Buddhist texts *Samantapasadika* and *Mahavamsa* suggest that Bindusara was a devotee of Brahmanism (historical Vedic religion), which was prevalent before the Maurya Empire. However, other records hint at Bindusara's connection with Jainism, Buddhism, and even the heterodox Ajivika. Ajivika was a fatalistic (*niyati*), determinist, and atheist religion that greatly appealed to the middle working classes. It died out in time and did not maintain the momentum that brought the religions of Jainism and Buddhism into the current era. If Bindusara adhered mostly to Ajivika, then any religious records relating to him would have been lost as these records were disappeared alongside the dissolution of Ajivika. However, there is a suggestion that Bindusara and his wife, Queen Subhadrangi (also mentioned as Queen Dharma or Queen Aggamahesi), were Brahmins of the Ajivika sect, putting them somewhere in between traditional Hinduism and Ajivika. There was a guru named Pingalavatsa (Janasana) who was associated with Bindusara and who was a Brahmin, and Bindusara is also accredited with making several donations to Brahmin monasteries (*Brahmana-bhatto*).

Chandragupta Maurya's infrastructure projects continued through Bindusara's reign and well into Ashoka's. The founder of the Mauryan Empire had invested heavily in buildings and systems that would support trade and agriculture in his kingdom. Chandragupta had built roads, irrigation systems, reservoirs, temples, and mines. He had ensured the extension and protection of trade routes, both on land and via water. Chandragupta, with the assistance of Chanakya, also ensured the supply of food and other resources to his army and to his subjects. He created a time of prosperity and showed a profound sense of civic duty. These practices were continued by his son, Bindusara, as well as his grandson, Ashoka.

The Mauryans were known as great road builders. Megasthenes attributes Chandragupta with the establishment of a highway from the capital of Pataliputra all the way west to Taxila. Records indicate that a road network spread from the capital in all directions to the edges of the empire, which facilitated the movement of the army as well as trade. There were many manufacturing centers, especially for weapons, and the Mauryans practiced state ownership and control, as well as public-private partnerships with independently owned entities. They garnered taxes from the trade and manufacturing processes and used these to further fund the economy, the social infrastructure, the army, and the bureaucratic system.

The might of Maurya was self-perpetuating. The emperors had an enclosed region, as it was bordered by the ocean or the Himalayas on many sides, which they could better dominate and control. However, the rulers of Maurya exercised their rulership diplomatically and in accordance with the Eastern concept of dharma (*dhamma*), or the right actions that lead to a virtuous life. They preferred negotiations over war but were always prepared to go to battle if necessary. The Mauryans required total allegiance to the Maurya monarchy but still invested heavily in broad-based social structures and the relief of suffering. Various major and minor religions flourished under their protectorate, but the Mauryan rulers were not averse to managing a diverse network of undercover spies to ensure their dominance was maintained.

The legends about Bindusara's personal situation (a multitude of wives and children—some sources claim that he had 101 sons with 16 women) are not entirely believable, but it is very likely that he had several wives and plenty of children. Most indigenous chronologies suggest that the man who eventually rose to take power from his father, Ashoka, was not the most likely candidate. It doesn't seem that he was the oldest, strongest, or even the favorite. Most records place Bindusara's death at approximately 273 BCE, after which there was a four-year struggle for succession. Whatever the true circumstances of the change in power were, the delay suggests there was at least some confusion regarding ascendancy.

Bindusara's twenty-four-year reign was the second of three extraordinarily lengthy rules. Maurya's continuation for almost a century and a half could well be attributed to the collective reigns of Chandragupta Maurya, Bindusara, and Ashoka, which collectively totaled almost ninety years. For ancient times, which were full of struggle and violence, three long reigns in a row were quite remarkable.

Chapter 5 – Imperial Unity under Ashoka the Great

Of Bindusara's many children, Ashoka (Asoka, Aśoka, or Ashoka the Great, also known as *Piyadasi* and *Devanampiya*) (c. 304– 232 BCE) had not been the obvious candidate for the throne. Ashoka's mother was Subhadrangi, and it is believed that she bore at least two of Bindusara's sons. Legends say that he murdered his rival siblings in order to take the throne for himself. This presumed infighting (whether it resulted in murder or not) accounts for the four-year gap between the end of Bindusara's reign and the beginning of Ashoka's. Several different legendary sources proclaim that Ashoka was fated to rule and that he was even predestined by the Hindu gods (*devatas*) as a great ruler before birth. Certain tales clarify that Ashoka had one main rival to the throne, his brother Susima (Sushima), who had not been successful in getting the area of Taxila under control when his father, Bindusara, died. Potentially, this failure, as well as Ashoka's successes in governing the northwest as an official royal viceroy, were what led to Ashoka's triumph over Susima. Legend also suggests that Susima was not popular amongst the courtiers, and although he was the legitimate heir to the throne, it was held for Ashoka instead. There is also the possibility that Bindusara peacefully handed over rulership after retiring!

[4] An artist's impression of Ashoka the Great, the third emperor of the Mauryan Empire of India, who ruled for almost four decades and spread the peaceful messages of Buddhism throughout the empire once he had turned from engaging in bloody warfare.

At first, Ashoka achieved dominance through warfare, continuing the bloody path of the ancestral lineage set by his father, Bindusara, and grandfather, Chandragupta Maurya. However, even though he had been raised a Hindu, his violent and empirical approach to expanding and maintaining the empire eventually gave way to the peaceful and non-violent way of Buddhism and the cosmically ordered way of *dhamma* (cosmic law or right action). *Dhamma*, or dharma, is a concept of several religions, including Buddhism, Hinduism, and other ascetic Indian religions. There isn't an exact translation for the concept of *dhamma* in Western languages, and even within traditional Indian religions, it has slightly different connotations.

Ashoka's reign began in c. 268 BCE, lasting for almost four decades until 232 BCE. His influence on the Mauryan Empire brought forth the golden age of Maurya, and he also extended and marked the boundaries of the realm at its most expansive. Spanning a geographical area of more than five million square kilometers across modern-day India and Iran (Persia), the Mauryan Empire existed as the largest geopolitical region the Indian subcontinent has ever known. This expansive empire boasted fifty-sixty million people at its zenith under the rulership of Ashoka.

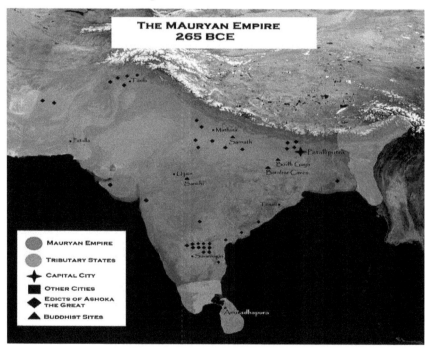

[5] The Mauryan Empire at its greatest extent, showing the capital in Magadha, Pataliputra, in the northeast and Taxila in the northwest. Maurya included most of modern-day India (except for the tip of the peninsula), as well as large tracts of modern-day Afghanistan, Bangladesh (Bengal), Bhutan, Iran, Nepal, Pakistan, and parts of China. Maurya covered an area of more than five million square kilometers (almost two million square miles).

The Buddhist manuscript, *Divyavadana*, describes Ashoka's mother (Subhadrangi) as the daughter of a Brahmin from present-day Bihar. Apparently, she was kept away from her husband due to palace intrigue until she had a son. Once she gave birth to a son, her position was elevated, and she could be closer to the king. She named her son Ashoka ("without sorrow.") Ashoka spent his childhood in the royal court, and as the potential heir to the throne, his days were full of hunting and lessons on statecraft. He was highly educated and even learned martial arts. As a teenager, Ashoka was given the monumental task of governing some of the outlying regions of the Mauryan Empire—Taxila (in Gandhara) and Ujjain (northwestern territories). His father, Bindusara, seems to have had great faith in him since he was about twenty years of age when he was sent out to deal with an uprising in Taxila. The populace was complaining about oppression by corrupt high officials. This was a very important region to the Mauryan Empire because it was highly prosperous and also on one of the main trade routes of the Uttarapatha (main central) highway that linked the capital of Pataliputra with the northwest. Ashoka marched an army of troops 1,500 kilometers (932 miles) northwest to deal with the uprising. He seems to have used his considerable powers of negotiation to quell the uprising and deal with the officials, and he is reported to have shown mercy to the people who laid down their arms. Ashoka was also made the governor of Malwa in Ujjain (central-western Maurya Empire), which was an important center of learning and trade. Ashoka's own rock edicts provide evidence that he (or another Mauryan prince) served as the viceroy in Ujjain.

It was while he was at Ujjain that Taxila revolted again. On this second occasion, his father, Bindusara, sent his other son, Susima, to deal with the uprising. Bindusara fell ill during the campaign and ordered Susima to be recalled. Legends tell, however, that Ashoka was the preferred candidate for regency at that time and that he returned to Pataliputra before his brother and was crowned (or crowned himself!) in his brother's absence upon Bindusara's death. Susima had still been in Taxila when Bindusara died and was delayed in returning. Some legends suggest that Bindusara had wanted to send Ashoka after his brother to Taxila, but through manipulation, Ashoka or Bindusara's ministers who favored Ashoka kept him in the capital so he could immediately ascend the throne upon Bindusara's death. There are legendary rumors that Ashoka had ninety-nine brothers and that he killed them all in order to ascend the throne, which is quite unlikely. Scholars suggest that he did have at least Susima and two other brothers killed, but they believe his youngest brother, Vitashoka, renounced any claim to the throne and became a Buddhist monk.

What is clear from the legends is that, at least politically, Ashoka was the favored candidate and that he was maneuvered into position by ministers according to their own agendas. Since there is a four-year gap between the end of Bindusara's reign and the beginning of Ashoka's, it is evident that not only was there a likely power struggle but also that the Pataliputra ministers had a long intercession in which to be in charge themselves. It may be that the succession to the Mauryan throne was purposefully obfuscated and delayed by Mauryan governors to allow themselves time to become more powerful and enforce their own ends. Also, although apocryphal evidence does not provide a factual account of Ashoka's life, the repetitious elements do suggest some truth or at least a widely accepted cultural belief system that may have been prevalent at the time. One of these elements was that Ashoka was destined to rule by the gods. He was considered a *chakravartin* (universal ruler). Not only did his influence extend throughout the extent of Maurya and to many territories beyond its borders, but he was also believed to be in charge of the *Yaksha* territory located above the earth and the *Naga* territory located below the earth.

There is evidence in Buddhist texts to suggest that Ashoka only ascended the throne in his thirties, meaning his role as a prince and viceroy of the outer territories was a long one. Once he was in position, Ashoka developed the palace and began using stone as the primary building material, most likely doing so with the assistance of foreign craftsmen. He began creating gardens and sculptures that disguised dark corners set aside for torture and plotting. Like most ancient rulers, the Mauryan emperors were autocrats and not sympathetic to anybody who challenged their rule. The empire was divided into four main provinces. The capitals were Tosali in the east, Taxila in the north, Ujjain in the west, and Suvarnagiri in the south. The emperor held absolute power and appointed officials to run all aspects of the state, as well as the large and pervasive espionage system. Buddhist texts suggest that Ashoka was both cruel and hedonistic before his conquest of Kalinga and his conversion to Buddhism. The pleasure-seeking Ashoka was known as "Kamashoka," the unkind Ashoka was "Chandashoka," and the enlightened spiritual Ashoka was "Dhammashoka."

There are very unpleasant legends of Ashoka's cruelty, but these cannot be verified and could potentially be inaccurate and unfair. Whatever barbarism Ashoka displayed upon his ascension and within the first decade of his rule, it was somewhat offset by his love for the people. His Rock Edict V refers to officers who were in charge of caring for his brothers' and sisters' families and all his other relatives. Ashoka's edicts consistently confirm his love for society, family, and community, and they state he was instrumental in keeping the social fabric of the community together and spreading family values. Although Buddhist texts like to greatly exaggerate Ashoka's change from despot to divine deliverer through the medium of Buddhism, it seems unlikely that Ashoka would have changed that much throughout his lifetime. It is perhaps more moderate to assume that he simply grew up, became more conscious of what conquering did to the world around him, and chose a different path. There is evidence that he was a sensible and level-headed young man, as well as a Buddhist, during his time as governor in Ujjain. The first decade of his reign in Pataliputra may have seen him wielding more power than usual and fulfilling his role according to the *Arthashastra*, but it is still very likely that he was at least a nominal Buddhist at this point in his life and that he already had wives and children. Ashoka's edicts express regret only over his success in the Kalinga War and don't reference more horrifying behavior as suggested in the Buddhist legends. Both his cruelty and the presumption of him being a divine leader seem to be an exaggeration.

At the beginning of his reign, Ashoka was guided by the *Arthashastra*, which followed the philosophical worldview of Charvaka—a completely material worldview devoid of supernatural events. The *Arthashastra* gives some insight into the seemingly dichotomous approach of the Mauryan emperors, who used bloody warfare, political subterfuge, and spiritual principles in equal measure. This treatise appears to give the king unlimited power to gain and maintain control according to his prerogative, and paradoxically, this control is condoned through the absolution of a higher power and the emperor's *dhamma*. The seven broad categories (limbs or *saptanga*) of rulership are listed in the *Arthashastra* as kingship, administration and governance (bureaucracy and the ministers), territory (including the population), defense and fortification (protection), treasury (including taxes), military and coercive authority (including subterfuge, spying, and warfare), and allies. Along with describing the mechanics of political strategy and general state manipulation, the *Arthashastra* provides some careful and frightful descriptions of how to poison people, how to light one's body on fire without getting burnt, and how to create an army of spies (including the use of honey traps as well as child monks)! It is clear that the first half-century of the Mauryan Empire was rife with intrigue, suspicion, and covert intelligence networks in order to maintain power. The seeds sown by the immoral but pragmatic Chanakya lasted for generations.

It seems that there was a system of committees that administered the lands from the capital in Pataliputra and that there was a hierarchal structure for each sub-region. The central revenue department ensured the collection of taxes and administration of the treasury. The military department was described by Megasthenes as having six subdivisions: navy, transport and provisions, foot soldiers, horses, chariots, and war elephants. The espionage department managed a network of secret agents, and the police department had headquarters in all major areas. There were jails as well as holding areas. The network of provincial and local administrators was comprised of magistrates, tax collectors, governors, accountants, and scribes.

The municipal administration included officials responsible for city administration, agriculture, markets, ships, tolls, iron and mining, and weights and measures. A municipal or city council was made up of thirty commissioners and was divided into six committees. The first committee was responsible for wages and provided goods; the second committee made arrangements for foreign dignitaries, tourists, and businessmen; the third committee kept records and registrations; the fourth committee looked after manufactured goods and the sale of commodities; the fifth committee regulated trade and related licenses and measurements; and the sixth committee collected taxes. There were also officers who assisted with infrastructure maintenance, socioeconomic affairs, and other civic responsibilities (including educational institutions). From the capital, foreign affairs were handled, as well as the census of births and deaths, industries, trade, manufacture, and taxes. Maurya was divided into smaller regions, which were overseen by a crown prince (*Yuvaraj*), a chief priest (*Purohita*), the commander-in-chief (*Senapati*), and the remaining civil servants (*Amatya*). The official head of a village was called a *Gramika*, and the official head of a town was a *Nagarika*. The head of a provincial administration was the royal prince (*Kumara*), who governed as the emperor's representative. The provincial royal princes were assisted by a council of ministers and the *dhamma-mahamattas* (the *dhamma* officers of morality instituted after Ashoka's conversion). The provincial hierarchy was repeated at an imperial level within the royal court of the capital.

The forested and tribal province of Kalinga (modern-day Odisha and some of Andhra Pradesh) in the northeast of the subcontinent had eluded both Ashoka's father and grandfather. Although they were surrounded by the Mauryan Empire (except for the Bay of Bengal to their east), the chieftains of Kalinga refused to subjugate themselves to Mauryan rule for over fifty years. When Ashoka took control, his first task was to conquer the resistant Kalinga region in order to make the Maurya Empire complete. In the seventh year of his reign (c. 261 BCE), Ashoka led Maurya to victory by waging one of the bloodiest battles India and the world have ever known. Up to 300,000 Indians lost their lives or were wounded (both soldiers and civilians), with many captured and enslaved. Hundreds of thousands of animals also lost their lives in the Kalinga War, which Ashoka ultimately deeply regretted. He also expressed regret over the pain, suffering, and disruption caused to holy people and regular people, as hundreds of thousands of Kalingas were deported or sold into slavery afterward.

Recent evidence indicates that on the eve of Ashoka's onslaught, Kalinga was organized into a number of prosperous urban nodes. The modern-day area of Sisupalgarh-Dhauli was the likely location of Ashoka's main point of attack. Ashoka's Dhauli edict a few kilometers from this point, as well as evidence of an ancient, pillared hall of stone monoliths (of palatial proportions), indicate that Dhauli was significant. According to excavations, it is likely that Sisupalgarh, which was one of the biggest cities in the world at the time, was one in a network of ancient cities that stretched for 400 kilometers (around 250 miles) along the Kalinga coast. They all had moats and were fortified. The urban nodes were also linked via a network of waterways. The Kalinga settlements were orderly, planned, well-situated, and wealthy. It is no wonder that Maurya needed to incorporate this independent state into its vastness, as the emperors needed their resources, wealth, and access to trade routes to maintain their pan-Indian empire.

However, the rulership of Kalinga before Ashoka's attack is mysterious. There are no records of a government or monarchy during the Mauryan era or even the preceding eras. Evidently, Kalinga was well governed and peaceful, and it was mentioned by Pliny the Elder as having tribes living close to the sea with a royal city. How they managed this extraordinary independence, tranquility, and affluence remains undocumented. The most likely solution is that Kalinga existed as a confederacy of tribal chiefs who worked toward a common cause and protected themselves as such. There appears to have been stability in Kalinga, and their nonchalance to the might of Maurya may have been the cause of Ashoka's determination to possess it. There is no absolute certainty as to where the Kalinga War was fought, but the most likely site is near Dhauli, overlooking the Daya River, which was said to have turned red with blood during the battle. However, the rock edicts in the vicinity do not mention the battle. An edict in Kandahar, thousands of kilometers away at the northwestern extremity of the Mauryan realm (in modern-day Afghanistan), has Ashoka relieving his conscience for the death, destruction, and mayhem he caused in taking Kalinga.

Ashoka's Rock Edict XIII:

Beloved-of-the-Gods, King Piyadasi [as Ashoka was referred to, and also "Devanampiya"], conquered the Kalingas eight years after his coronation. One hundred and fifty thousand were deported, one hundred thousand were killed and more died [from other causes]. After the Kalingas had been conquered, Beloved-of-the-Gods came to feel a strong inclination towards the Dhamma and for instruction in Dhamma. Now Beloved-of-the-Gods feels deep remorse for having conquered the Kalingas. Indeed Beloved-of-the-Gods is deeply pained by the killing, dying and deportation that take place when an unconquered country is conquered...the killing, death or deportation of a hundredth, or even a thousandth part of those who died during the conquest of Kalinga now pains Beloved-of-the-Gods. Now Beloved-of-the-Gods thinks that even those who do wrong should be forgiven where forgiveness is possible.

Once Ashoka the Great acquired Kalinga, he made it part of his Mauryan dominion, establishing a fortification within the conquered lands and eventually its own system of government that adhered to the Mauryan civil hierarchy. Ashoka held the largest extent ever covered by the sprawling Mauryan Empire, but in time, he regretted it deeply. Despite Ashoka's remorse, Kalinga remained under Mauryan rulership throughout Ashoka's reign and was divided into a northern and southern section with Dhauli (ancient Tosali) as the capital of the north. Unusually, the subjugation of the Kalinga region was the catalyst for Ashoka's conversion to Buddhism, which took place eleven years after he took power. The bloodshed and enslavement of the people during the Kalinga War convinced Ashoka that there must be another way to geopolitical and cultural unification. Although legends suggest that he experienced an epiphany on the battlefield after the Kalinga War, it is most likely that his full conversion to non-violence and adherence to the gentle ways of *dhamma* happened more gradually over the years. It is also unclear whether Emperor Ashoka was already acquainted with Buddhism before Kalinga and simply began adhering to it more or if he only discovered Buddhism after the devastation of his final battle. If the legends of his love connection to Devi (his first wife) at Sanchi during his governance of Ujjain are correct, then he was acquainted with Buddhism before the Kalinga War. As mentioned above, the most reasonable conclusion is that Ashoka was a nominal Buddhist before the Kalinga massacre but was changed by his experience of the war and began transitioning to a practicing Buddhist after the war.

Buddhism was founded sometime between the 6th and early 4th century BCE by an ancient Indian enlightened master who became known as the Buddha (Siddhartha Gautama), who was a part of a long line of divinely chosen Buddhas. The Buddha taught peace through the creation of inner discipline and the relief of suffering by abnegating human desire. The Buddha described an eight-fold path to inner holiness through the practice of "rightness" in all human thought and behavior. He preached that through meditation, discourse, humility, and self-denial, humanity could reach a peaceful state known as nirvana. The pillars of the Buddha's teachings have been encapsulated as the Four Noble Truths, which describe the human condition of suffering and the path through suffering to enlightenment. In time, Buddha's teachings spread throughout central and eastern Asia by monks who traveled and taught these truths.

Ashoka began instituting the life-enhancing (*ahimsa*) ways of Buddhism into the royal court and into his administration of the empire. He used Buddhism and the concept of *dhamma* as his state policy in a new and exceptionally inspiring form of kingship. He wanted to rule his conquered world through love and faith and by preventing all cruelty to humans and animals alike. The Kalinga massacre had left hundreds of thousands of his people displaced or in servitude under hard labor. Part of Ashoka's deepening spirituality was to end all forms of slavery and indentured labor. He also put a ban on unnecessary hunting and any violent sports, including humans and animals alike, notoriously banning the killing of almost all animals in his royal kitchens for curries. He did allow a few choice animals to be killed each year for special occasions. Ashoka gave up conquest entirely and instead made pilgrimages to holy Buddhist sites, encouraging those he met to practice tolerance and humanity. He sent Buddhist emissaries in the form of male and female monks throughout the Indian subcontinent as well as farther afield (as far as the Mediterranean and Egypt in the west and south Asia in the east) to spread the word of Buddhism and perform rites for those who wished to convert.

Certain historians promulgate that there was a distinct difference between Ashoka's application of *dhamma* and his Buddhist inclinations, suggesting that his concept of *dhamma* was very simplistic and disconnected from the intricacies of being a practicing ascetic. Ashoka's concept of *dhamma* related to generalized standards of behavior and moral attitudes that were thought to be drawn from both Hindu Brahmanism and Buddhist teachings. Ashoka himself was both a monk and a monarch during his reign, and he not only promulgated the policy of *dhamma* but also perpetually strove to embody it. His messages to his subjects were designed to increase general social responsibility, equality, and tolerance. In accordance with the balanced, non-interfering, and non-attached concept of *dhamma*, Ashoka did not enforce his lofty ideals but rather spread edicts to persuade and enlighten his people.

Although the spread of Buddhism might not seem revolutionary today, it must be remembered that at the time of Ashoka's reign, it was a heterodox (outside of the orthodox Brahmanism of the Hindu religion) and obscure religion. It was Ashoka who helped Buddhist principles to gain traction in Asia and eventually in Southeast Asia, where it is prevalent today. Brahmans had acquired considerable power in previous generations through their control of ritualistic practices and the acquisition of resources in the form of payments for spiritual services. Still, there were many tribal areas that did not practice any of the major religions but rather believed in localized traditions. The vast expanse of the Mauryan Empire was a melting pot of religions and spiritual beliefs, and the emperor used edicts to create a common and unbiased language of unity and harmony. Ashoka's edicts did not aim to convert his subjects but rather to create an atmosphere of tolerance and trust in support of national harmony.

[6] A 1ˢᵗ century BCE/CE stone relief from Sanchi (a north-central Buddhist site) of Emperor Ashoka Maurya (Piyadasi) on his chariot visiting the Nagas (supernatural beings) at Ramagrama (holy Nepalese Buddhist site).

Ashoka believed in the everyday practices of honesty, compassion, truthfulness, mercy, benevolence, and the application of "many good deeds," amongst other virtues, which he included in his edicts. Interestingly, Ashoka's proclamations did not extol particular philosophies or religious dictates and methods of worship. Furthermore, he was tolerant of all of Maurya's religions and did not insist that the people convert or believe in Buddhism. The emperor traveled to preach in the rural areas of his dominions about the Buddhist belief system and advocated the equalizing of social hierarchies and the fair dispensation of punishments.

Ashoka's newfound path of peacefulness meant he ruled with mercy and justice, and he sought to institute laws that benefited everyone and not just the upper echelons of society. In his thirteenth regnal year (c. 255 BCE), Ashoka used the established civil servant network and designated some of the high officers as "dhamma ministers," who were employed to administer over the particularly weak and outlying communities of the realm. These *dhamma-mahamattas* were specifically employed to teach and enforce the rules of *dhamma* to the general population. In a revolutionary move, Ashoka the Great advocated against cruelty to animals, even going so far as to ban hunting and commission animal hospitals. Ashoka's aim was to relieve the suffering of all living things under his command; however, at the same time, this unusual leader retained his army, slaves, and the inherited attitude of sovereignty over an expansive dominion. Ashoka held Maurya peacefully but firmly for the remainder of his rule.

Pataliputra, the capital of the empire, reached the pinnacle of its splendor and fame during Ashoka's reign. During its height, Pataliputra stretched for 15 kilometers (nine miles) along the Ganges River, with a width of 2.5 kilometers (1.5 miles). The perimeter of Pataliputra measured 35 kilometers (22 miles). It was shaped like a parallelogram, and it had a surface area of 25 square kilometers (15.5 miles). (The perimeter of ancient Rome measured 14 kilometers—8.5 miles—at its maximum.) Most importantly, Ashoka introduced stone as a building material rather than the wood of his ancestors. When Ashoka turned to Buddhism, he built monasteries and erected pillars with his edicts within the capital. Pataliputra is recognized as the birthplace of Buddhism. Its reputation as the "City of Flowers" was enhanced by Greco-Roman writers, such as Aelian (Roman author, c. 175–235 AD), who described Indian palaces as being far superior to those of Persia, with parks full of tame peacocks. Ashoka, in particular, was known as a great builder and likely imported foreign craftsmen during his establishment of the capital. Relics of Persian influences from the architecture of the Mauryan period confirm the likelihood of foreign craftsmen being used, particularly after the fall of the Achaemenid Empire after its conquest by Alexander the Great.

During the Mauryan period, Pataliputra was one of the largest cities in the world, with a population of between 150,000 and 400,000 people. Pataliputra had been established as a small fort town in approximately 500 BCE by the Magadhan ruler Udayin. The water fort (*jaldurga*) was built at the confluence of the Ganges, Gandaki, and Son Rivers. After the fall of the Mauryan Empire, it continued to be a vital capital for subsequent dynasties, such as the Gupta (c. 320–550 CE) and the Pala (c. 750–1200 CE). Pataliputra's strategic positioning in the center of northeast India at the confluence of these three rivers ensured its domination over riverine trade across the Indo-Gangetic Plain. In addition, it became a powerful center for commerce and learning. During Chandragupta Maurya's reign, the palace of Pataliputra had been a group of several buildings, including a large, pillared hall. Eighty pillars, seven meters high, were arranged in rows, dividing the hall into a number of smaller bays. According to Megasthenes, the gilded pillars were adorned with golden vines and silver birds. The buildings were situated in an expansive park filled with fish ponds and embellished with ornamental trees and shrubs. During Ashoka's period, much of the wood architecture was replaced with stone, and the art and architecture received the Mauryan polish treatment that made it shine like a mirror. Archaeological evidence has produced lofty stone pillars, lion thrones, other colossal figures, and exquisite railings (ornate fences and gateways) for the Buddhist stupas (mound-like structures built for worship and meditation). Ashoka's reign marked the beginning of the Buddhist school of architecture.

By the end of Ashoka's reign, he governed the entire area of the Indian subcontinent extending from the Bay of Bengal in the east up to and including the Hindu Kush (Afghanistan) in the west, as well as the modern-day areas of Bangladesh (former Bengal), Nepal, Bhutan, Pakistan, and parts of China and Iran. It was only the southern tip of the Indian Peninsula (modern-day Tamil Nadu and Kerala) that was not under his rule. At the height of the Mauryan Empire, political unity and military security ensured a broad-based economic system that benefited trade, commerce, and agriculture. The petty tribal squabbles of the pre-Mauryan period, in which internecine warfare had prevented the establishment of a single cultural and economic hegemony, had given rise to Chanakya's original vision—one of a united pan-Indian superpower with a disciplined central authority. The Mauryan army created internal peace and economic security by getting rid of gangs of robbers, local private armies, and any chieftains that threatened the overarching power of Maurya. Local industries and individuals were required to pay homage and taxes to the Mauryan regency, but history indicates that this was to their long-term benefit, as well as that of Maurya, in terms of the economy, personal safety, and social security. The sense was that as long as all regions and peoples within the empire submitted to Maurya's beneficent imperial domination, all would be well.

Chapter 6 – Consolidation of Maurya: The Edicts of Ashoka

It is not precisely known why Ashoka specifically chose Buddhism as his spiritual path except that he had made an association with the Buddhist monks Upagupta and Moggaliputta Tissa, who may have been the same person, and was also inspired by a male monk named Nigrodha (Nyagrodha), whose tranquil and fearless appearance impressed him. (Texts suggest another male monk named Samudra.) Apocryphal evidence states that Nigrodha taught Ashoka a lesson on earnestness (*appamada*), which prompted Ashoka to seek further teachings on Buddhism. He became an *upasaka* of Buddhism (an advocate who does not take the vows of a monk or nun; in other words, a devout lay follower). It was during regular visits to the Buddhist monastery Kukkutarama at Pataliputra that he met and became an adherent of the practicing monk Moggaliputta Tissa, moving deeper into Buddhism through his temple visits. Ashoka most likely chose Buddhism because he seemed to be looking for an applicable life philosophy, including a way of being that he could simultaneously apply to rulership. The equally passive, deeply spiritual, and non-violent ways of Jainism may have been too ascetic to practice and simultaneously rule as the emperor. Buddhism provided an abundance of spiritual teachings and an entire universal philosophy conducive to those who could not become a monk or a nun—this belief system seemed more appropriate for Ashoka, who remained a highly involved and attentive ruler for the remainder of his life.

Regardless of which monk first inspired Ashoka, he clearly had an abundance of Buddhist influences around him and is thought to have had a succession of Buddhist teachers. There is also a legend that tells of Ashoka falling in love with a merchant's daughter, Devi (also known as Vedisa- or Vidisha-Mahadevi), who lived near Sanchi (the site of an important Buddhist temple complex) at Besnagar (modern-day Vidisha). Sanchi was a north-central hilltop area on the way to the capital of Ujjain, Avanti, to which Ashoka had been assigned to govern in his youth. It is rumored that Devi was a Buddhist (and also possibly a princess of Ujjain) and that she was instrumental in Ashoka's conversion to Buddhism. Other Buddhist sources suggest she was a descendant of Gautama Buddha and belonged to the spiritual Shakya clan. Records suggest that Devi became Ashoka's wife along with at least two others—Asandhimitra and Karuvaki—but he possibly could have had up to four different wives. Records suggest that Ashoka's son, Mahinda, was ordained into Buddhism at the age of twenty when his father had been on the throne for six years. This would mean that Ashoka was married and producing heirs well before his reign as emperor and that he was also likely a Buddhist well before he ascended the throne. Devi may have introduced Ashoka to Buddhism, but it is also possible that he was already an adept of Buddhism when he met her and that they simply shared a love for it together. Buddhism was a minor heterodox sect at that time in India, along with Jainism, Ajivika, and Charvaka, and vied with the mainstream orthodox *Sanatan Dharma* ("Eternal Order") of Hinduism.

Some of the main sources of information for the Mauryan period come from Buddhist texts, such as the *Mahavamsa* (a 5th-century CE Sri Lankan chronicle written in Pali by a Buddhist monk) and the *Dipavamsa* (the 4th-century CE "Chronicle of the Island"—this is the oldest historical record of Sri Lanka). These documents mention

Buddhist missions sent to Sri Lanka by Ashoka, including an important visit by his daughter, Theri Sangamitta. The 2nd-century CE Buddhist "Narrative of Ashoka" (the *Ashokavadana*, which is a part of the greater *Divyavadana*) includes legends about Ashoka and his role in spreading Buddhism, as does the Jatakas (dated c. 300 BCE–c. 400 CE), which is a voluminous compendium of poems and prose that assist with depicting the socioeconomic conditions in India at the time. However, caution must be applied when referencing these works because the writers were not contemporaries of Ashoka's day. The religious texts were written in retrospect by adherents of the faith who heralded Ashoka as a great Buddhist king.

Ashoka continued the establishment of Buddhism in his empire through over forty edicts, which can be found throughout modern-day India, Nepal, Pakistan, Bangladesh, and Afghanistan. These edicts were either written on tall, polished sandstone pillars or on cave walls, stone slabs, and stones in Prakrit or other local languages closely associated with Sanskrit (Brahmi, Magadhi, Kharosthi, and even Aramaic and Greek). Ashoka strategically positioned these edicts at religious places, at intersections, and along byways where many people would see them and even repeated some of the edicts, such as number XIII, which was his regret over conquering Kalinga. Many of the edicts still survive today and describe his ascetic life as a non-violent Buddhist committed to the moral and peaceful leadership of his people. The edicts describe the reforms he made as a leader and his wish for the Mauryan people to follow his example, but they do not describe the philosophies of Buddhism, nor did they attempt to convert his people to his religion.

Instead, the edicts encouraged people to emulate Ashoka's newfound spiritual approach and to take responsibility for their actions. His new foundation of leadership through righteousness placed the moral and spiritual wellbeing of his people first. Through his edicts, Ashoka dispensed advice like the Buddha before him. In general, Ashoka's edicts can be separated into four categories: major and minor rock edicts and major and minor pillar edicts. The following edicts attributed to Ashoka have been unearthed throughout the Mauryan Empire: fourteen major rock edicts expounding the principles of *dhamma*; two Kalinga (Odisha) rock edicts describing a new administration after the Kalinga War; minor rock edicts describing Ashoka's conversion to Buddhism, as well as his personal history and more on *dhamma*; thirteen pillar edicts (major and minor), which act as appendices to the rock edicts and further propose Buddhism and *dhamma*; and three cave edicts describing Ashoka's tolerant attitude (at Barabar Caves, the oldest surviving rock-cut caves in India).

In general, the minor edicts are religious and expound Buddhism, while the major edicts are moral and political and speak more broadly of *dhamma*. While the minor edicts go into some detail regarding Buddhism, such as mentioning Buddha (and previous Buddhas before him) and details regarding the Buddhist communities and scriptures, the major edicts never mention Buddhism and are far more concerned with establishing law and order throughout the Maurya Empire. The major edicts were spread widely to the extents of Maurya, while the minor edicts were centered in mainland India, with many in the south or along the edges of Kalinga. All of the pillar edicts (major and minor) were located in central northern India at the site of Buddhist monasteries and other holy places, specifically in the modern-day Indian states of Bihar, Uttar Pradesh, Madhya Pradesh, and Haryana. Some of the Ashokan pillars do not have edicts. (The discrepancy in content of writings and geographical location, as well as the fact that the major edicts are far superior in quality, has led some scholars to believe that the major and minor edicts were not necessarily created by the same ruler, but this is a topic of debate.)

Records state that Ashoka began establishing his edicts to spread the idea of *dhamma* in his twelfth regnal year. His officers were already employed in five-year-long inspection tours of their specific jurisdictions, which included the spread of *dhamma*. The fourteen major rock edicts are fascinating in their content, as they include the prohibition of animal sacrifices; measures of social welfare and infrastructural development; respect for Brahmins, Sramanas (ascetic laborers), and elders; the *dhamma mahamattas* (*dhamma* ministers) and their duties; religious tolerance; *Dhammayatras* (evangelizing missions and tours); the abolition of meaningless ceremonies and rituals; the use of *dhamma* rather than war in conquest; *dhamma* policy; the Kalinga War; and inspiring people to lead a religious life. Overall, Ashoka's messages were of love, tolerance, piety, discipline, and the elimination of cruelty to others and superstition.

As an example, the Rock Edict VI of Ashoka states:

> Beloved-of-the-Gods speaks thus: twelve years after my coronation I started to have Dhamma edicts written for the welfare and happiness of the people, and so that not transgressing them they might grow in the Dhamma. Thinking: "How can the welfare and happiness of the people be secured?" I give my attention to my relatives, to those dwelling far, so I can lead them to happiness and then I act accordingly. I do the same for all groups. I have honored all religions with various honors. But I consider it best to meet with people personally.

Chronologically, the first inscription of Ashoka's was the bilingual (Greek and Aramaic) rock inscription in Kandahar (modern-day Afghanistan), upon which he professes his support of Buddhism and provides an impressive list of foreign destinations to which he sent envoys. This rock inscription was dated to have been written approximately ten years into his reign and two and a half years after the Kalinga War. Interestingly, the classical Greek inscription uses the word *Eusebeia* (piety) as the translation for *dhamma*, while the Aramaic word used is *Qsyt* (truth). The leaders and locales to which emissaries were sent are listed as Antiochus Theos, King of Syria and western Asia; Ptolemy Philadelphos, King of Egypt; Magas, King of Cyrene (Libya); Antigonos Gonatas, King of Macedonia; and

Alexander, King of Epirus (Greece and Albania). Rock Edict V adds to the impressive list of nations above, as it included the Rashtrikas of the Maratha country (south and west India) and the Gandharas of the Peshawar frontier (Pakistan). The edicts were located as far west as Afghanistan and as far south as Andhra Pradesh (almost at the bottom reaches of the Maurya Empire), as well as north around Taxila. These artifacts describe the frontiers of the Mauryan Empire as being the territories of the Greeks (the northwestern trans-Indus Valley of the Seleucid Empire) and the Kambojas and the Gandharas (far northern tribes of the Indian subcontinent). The edicts accurately locate Greece as being 6,500 kilometers (about 4,400 miles) away from the center of Maurya.

Although the edicts of Ashoka are taken for granted today, they remained hidden after the fall of the Mauryan Empire until the 19th century, when British archaeologists, historians, and antiquarians made it their purpose to uncover and understand them. The edicts specifically were deciphered by James Prinsep (1799– 1840) in 1837 CE. Prinsep was a British scholar, orientalist, philologist, archaeologist, and an official of the British East India Company. He uncovered a script at the Sanchi Stupa referring to Ashoka as "Beloved-of-the-Gods," a previously unknown reference. Credit also goes to British officers and administrators during Britain's colonial domination of India, as they noticed that the extent and proliferation of these edicts were of exceptional historical value. Over the next few decades, more artifacts that clearly belonged to the same time period were uncovered, but it was only in 1915 that an edict referring specifically to "Ashoka" was found. This was when historians could confirm that the entirety of Mauryan edicts belonged to Ashoka the Great. From Girnar (western Gujarat) to Kandahar (modern-day Afghanistan), from Sopara in the Deccan Plateau to Mysore in the south (Karnataka), the enormity and impact of Ashoka's reign could not be ignored. At last, the references made to a remarkable leader who had converted to Buddhism in ancient Buddhist texts and other scriptural documentation, such as the *Mahavamsa*, the *Divyavadana*, and the *Ashokavadana*, could be confirmed as one ruler: Ashoka.

[7] A major rock edict from Shahbazgarhi, Pakistan. Two large rock edicts were cut into boulders in the Vale of Peshawar. The edicts represent some of the first writing in south Asia and are written from right to left in the Kharosthi script. The edicts speak of Ashoka's dhamma, *or "righteous law," and are located beside one of the ancient trade routes connecting Taxila in the southeast to the Valley of Peshawar (east of the Khyber Pass connecting Pakistan to Afghanistan) and other northern territories.*

The rock and minor edicts were created soon after Ashoka's conquest of Kalinga, and five of the thirteen discovered minor pillar edicts were completed in approximately the thirteenth year of Ashoka's reign. However, the remaining eight (or more) major pillar edicts are thought to have been created in the twenty-sixth and twenty-seventh years of his reign, and their inscriptions are considerably more detailed and extensive than any of the minor edicts. Ashoka referred to his own major pillars as *Dhamma thambha*, or "pillars of the Dharma," and they almost act as appendices to the shorter statements of the minor edicts. Standing between forty and fifty feet high (twelve to fifteen meters) and weighing up to fifty tons, the pillars were quarried at Chunar or Mathura in the northern part of India and west of Pataliputra as single stone monoliths. The pillars were dragged—sometimes hundreds of miles—to their locations to be erected. These monoliths were carefully crafted in beautifully reflective polished stone and adorned with Buddhist and regal symbols and animals, and they were topped with stone capitals in a separate and often different piece of stone. Most of the tops (capitals) of the pillars are of animals sympathetic to the Buddhist belief system, and they were placed upon an inverted lotus flower—a poignant symbol of Buddhism. The lotus is usually topped by a lion, although elephants and a zebu (humped) bull in a standing or seated position have been found. (Ancient Chinese reports also state there were horse capitals.) The lion is a pervasive symbol of Buddhism since the Buddha was born into the Shakya or lion clan. The lion, of course, is also a symbol of leadership and royalty, and the animals were similarly carved from a single piece of stone.

The surviving capitals are some of India's most remarkable historical and artistic artifacts. Some of these exquisite sculptures form the basis of the Indian Republic's official regalia—specifically the wheel and the four outward-pointing lions. The edicts were inscribed on the pillars in local dialects so they could be understood by as many people as possible. Even though many of the pillars are broken, the condition of the pillars and capitals have survived centuries in the elements. There is confusion over exactly how many pillars there were, but up to twenty are thought to have survived, with seven still intact. The rock edicts are typically found where large flat rocks were available for inscriptions. The pillar edicts were more placed to not only mark certain extents of the Mauryan Empire at a particular point in time but also to mark important Buddhist locations, such as Lumbini (Nepal), the birthplace of the Buddha. This pillar's inscription commemorates Ashoka's pilgrimage to that place. Other edicts were strategically placed in urban nodes or along busy highways in order to be read by as many people as possible.

Ashoka's architecture and edicts were created in the Hinayana Buddhist period (6th BCE to 1st century CE) in which there aren't representations of the Buddha but rather the symbols of Buddhism. The choice of a pillar as a structure is also noteworthy because, in both Buddhism and Hinduism, the pillar is thought to represent the axis (*axis mundi*) on which the world spins. Ashoka's edifices represent some of the first physical representations of the Buddhist religion. Ashoka's most famous pillar is at Sarnath (c. 250 BCE) in the northern state of Uttar Pradesh. Sarnath is a location of profound Buddhist spirituality. To this day, it remains a destination for Buddhist pilgrims, and in Ashoka's day, it was a place of monasteries (viharas) and learning. Sarnath is thought to be the location where the Buddha gave his first sermon and described the Four Noble Truths of Buddhism after he gained enlightenment. The Buddha was said to have attained enlightenment under the Bodhi Tree in Bodh Gaya—a religious site in the northeastern Bihar state. An existing polished sandstone slab (the Vajrasana or "Diamond Throne") still exists under the ancient Bodhi Tree, which is thought to have been installed by Ashoka at the place where the Buddha gained enlightenment. The empty throne is not meant to be occupied but rather serves as a *cetiya* ("holy relic") of where the Buddha once sat. The sandstone slab is decorated on its sides by flame palmettes, rosettes, lotuses, and geese, and geometric patterns were carved into the top. It is reminiscent of some of Ashoka's pillar capitals. Alongside the *Vajrasana* are the remnants of an ancient Buddhist temple, which has also been attributed to Ashoka. Bodh Gaya was known as Sambodhi ("Complete Enlightenment") in ancient times, and Ashoka is thought to have visited it in his tenth regnal year.

Ashoka invested heavily in the development of monuments and monasteries at Sarnath after his conversion, including a large meditation dome (stupa) called Dharmarajika Stupa, complete with a megalithic railing. Ashoka also installed a monolithic pillar topped with a lion capital. Ashoka's seven-foot-tall capital is divided into three sections. A Buddhist lotus forms the foundation of the capital, upon which rests a cylindrical abacus. Four animals represent the cardinal directions of the abacus: a horse, a lion, a bull, and an elephant. They are all separated by the wheel of *dhamma* (progress along the righteous path). The capital is topped by four powerful outward-pointing lions, which are also facing the cardinal directions; they symbolize courage, confidence, and pride. These lions are said to represent Ashoka's power over all the land. The capital has been used as India's official emblem since the 1950s and also appears on banknotes and coins. The pillar was inscribed in the Brahmi script and warned monks and nuns from causing divisions in the Sangha (Buddhist community). Sarnath is a profound example of the evolution of Buddhism in India over one and a half millennium and also provides a priceless historical heritage for the Mauryan age.

[8] Some of the surviving or reproduced edicts of Ashoka: The lion capitals (sculptural edifices topping the pillars); the Dharma Wheel (Ashoka Chakra); and pillars inscribed with his edicts.

Unfortunately, some of Ashoka's pillars are in pieces, with the capitals set aside in museums. In certain places, reconstructions now stand where the pillars once stood. Along with the edicts, Ashoka created Buddhist shrines, temples, and monasteries and sent missionaries to foreign lands. Much of the spread of Buddhism to Eastern countries is attributed to Ashoka's missionary work. Ashoka also abolished the caste (social class) system and preached equality. More than 2,000 years later, many of the monuments still stand and give insight into the Mauryan story.

Ashoka's Pillar Edict II describes *dhamma* (right action), which consists of performing good deeds and practicing compassion, liberality, truthfulness, and purity. Overall, *dhamma* in the context in which Ashoka instituted it was essentially "good conduct" or "decent overall behavior." He also became a strict vegetarian and eventually converted the palace to vegetarianism while advocating for the prevention of cruelty to animals or unnecessary animal sacrifices. Through his edicts, Ashoka preached respect for elders, teachers, and parents, as well as tolerance and respect for all other religions. In an unprecedented move atypical of his era of conquest and domination, he spoke of the necessity of comfort and plenty for all living creatures within his dominions.

Ashoka is referred to in his edicts as "Devanampiya Piyadasi" ("Beloved-of-the-Gods" and "Gracious of Men"). The Buddhist texts, from which we get much of the information about his life, refer to him as a model of virtuous behavior. Ashoka stressed the emptiness of the Indian ritualistic way of life, which could be overly ceremonious and flamboyant. He urged the practice of *dhamma*, for he believed correct action in just the right amounts proved most beneficial in both this life and the next. Ashoka's Pillar Edict V describes how he regularly released prisoners from jail and introduced a fairer judicial system. He preached equality above all else—within humanity, in social status, throughout religious practices, and across cultures and regions. In contrast to the caste system that had been entrenched throughout India, and in spite of his lofty royal lineage and position, he encouraged generosity to the poor.

Ashoka conformed with the Buddha's advice from the *Anguttara Nikaya* (Buddhist discourses) in creating no harm and living in moderation. Ashoka desired that people be well versed in other's religions and practice kind treatment of one another. He promoted kindness, self-examination, truthfulness, gratitude, purity of heart, enthusiasm, loyalty, self-control, and the love of *dhamma*. Ashoka's practice of Buddhist *dhamma* sought to uphold a form of cosmic law and order on Earth. His edicts have a distinctly personal tone, unlike the typical official declarations of his day, and they provide insight into the character of this complex and fascinating man. His messages are sincere and simple but perhaps a little repetitive and condescending at times. Ashoka's edicts assure the populace that he thinks of them as his children and that their welfare is his foremost priority. He pledges to foreign lands that he has no intention of conquering them.

Unfortunately, there is no way of knowing how successful Ashoka's edicts were. He is the first world leader attributed with instituting a national Buddhist polity and is heralded, even today, as an ideal to be followed. If the reforms were effective, it is also uncertain how widely the new peaceful regime spread or how long it lasted. Ashoka's written wish was that his spiritual style of governance needed to be upheld by his successors, but he also states that this could not be done without significant effort. It was unlikely that any empire could have produced successors who'd have had the political will and commitment to follow through with his unique vision.

Certain scholars are not convinced that all of the pillar and rock edicts came from one Mauryan ruler since the same name is not used upon all of the messages. Ashoka's name only technically appears on the minor rock edicts, whereas "Piyadasi" or "Devanampiya Piyadasi" ("Beloved-of-the-Gods") appears on the major rock edicts and the major pillar edicts. This evidence may suggest that two different rulers were responsible for the edicts. The Piyadasi king only speaks of *dhamma*, while Ashoka refers specifically to Buddhism. The Piyadasi edicts are widespread, as they could be found up to and including the boundaries of the Seleucid Empire in the northwest, which represents the greatest extent Maurya ever achieved. However, the edicts specifically attributed to Ashoka are centered within mainland India. The two sets of inscriptions are also of vastly different quality, with the major edicts of the outer limits being far superior. There is also a possibility that Bindusara was responsible for the original set of edicts that extended farther, but this is still uncertain.

Ashoka's Buddhist edicts do provide solid evidence that he was a committed and practicing Buddhist, one who took the purity and authenticity of his faith seriously. Several of his rock edicts specify behaviors and teachings that would keep the Sangha (Buddhist community) learned and united. The Sri Lankan Buddhist tradition attributes Ashoka with expelling a huge number of false monks from Pataliputra and organizing the Third Buddhist Council. He goes on to compile an orthodox Buddhist text with the monk Moggaliputta-Tissa to prevent any future infiltration of falsity into the order. The irony in this situation is that the creation and infiltration of false monks may have been caused by Ashoka's widespread influence and perpetuation of Buddhism throughout Maurya. It was as if he was spreading a homogenous belief system but also needed to be the overlord of how that system was practiced within his realm.

There is documentation that Ashoka had at least four sons (Mahinda or Mahendra, Tivara or Tivala, Kunala, and Taluka) and two daughters (Sanghamitra or Sanghamitta and Charumati), some of whom became instrumental as Buddhist envoys on pilgrimages to the outer limits of his territories as well as into foreign lands. Legends say that he had two children with his most well-known wife Devi—Mahinda and Sanghamitra—and that these two children were the most influential in his Buddhist missions, even becoming Buddhist monks and nuns themselves in the sixth year of Ashoka's reign. Sanghamitra was sent as far as Sri Lanka, where tales of her mission were recorded in the *Mahavamsa*. Indigenous traditions state that both siblings were requested by the Sri Lankan King Devanampiya Tissa to visit and spread Buddhism throughout his land. Devanampiya was said to have been a contemporary of Ashoka's. Rumor suggests that Sanghamitra planted a branch from the sacred Bodhi Tree in the ancient capital of Anuradhapura, where it is worshipped to this day. Sanghamitra was supposedly sent to Sri Lanka to establish an order of nuns, but legends tell that King Devanampiya Tissa was so taken with Buddhist ideals that he converted to Buddhism and then instituted it as the state religion, where it remains the primary religion today (70 percent of the population are practicing Buddhists).

Megasthenes wrote that polygamy was widely practiced amongst the royal classes of India at that time, and Ashoka was no exception, as there are five documented wives of Ashoka (Devi, Asandhimitra, Karuvaki, Tishyarakshita, and Padmavati), although these names cross traditions, meaning some might refer to the same person. For instance, Tishyarakshita may have been the royal name of Karuvaki. Karuvaki is the only queen of Ashoka's that he mentions in his inscriptions. He describes her, along with his son Tivara, on his pillar edict at Allahabad as making generous religious donations. Devi is not mentioned on official edicts, and legend suggests that she chose to remain at her birthplace close to the Buddhist center of Sanchi near Vidisha rather than move to Pataliputra. Other tales clarify that although she had two children by Ashoka, they never actually married but rather retained a close association through their belief in Buddhism.

Ashoka sent both written and oral messages abroad in support of Buddhism. These Buddhist missions, known as *Dhammayatras*, included five states of the Greek kings, the kingdoms of Cholas and Pandyas (southern India), Ceylon (Sri Lanka), and Suvarnabhumi (Burma), as well as parts of Southeast Asia and China. Ashoka is also thought to have sent emissaries as far as North Africa (Egypt and Libya). These international tours were not only important for spreading the idea of *dhamma* but were also important for cultural and trade relations. Ashoka also undertook his own pilgrimages to sites sacred to the Buddha and traveled his kingdom to ensure the construction of his edicts and to personally share the word of Buddhism. It is not known how Ashoka's missionaries were trained or prepared in undertaking the substantial (and dangerous) task of spreading Buddhism throughout the realm and farther afield. Naturally, they would have met with a myriad of other faiths as well as skeptics who would not be certain of this burgeoning religion of the

Mauryan king. The Buddhist missionaries would have needed to prove their worth and provide some evidence of their superior qualities. The dispensation of Buddhism was not simply a didactic task, for the monks would have sought to create definitive and lasting Buddhist colonies, as many were probably away from home for a long time or possibly forever.

Buddhist teachings, such as the *Mahavamsa*, describe the Buddhist emissaries (including Ashoka's son) using considerable supernatural powers to influence others. While the supernatural might be hard to believe, it is possible that the monks had developed talents that took their vassals by surprise and persuaded them to join the Buddhist community. However, in many cases, it is most likely that any conversions to Buddhism came about after long periods of teaching Buddhist law and other principles of moral behavior. Interestingly, according to the final ordinations recorded as per apocryphal evidence, more women converted to Buddhism than men. Since Ashoka is thought to have sent his daughter Sanghamitra (a practicing Buddhist nun) to dispense Buddhism as far as Sri Lanka, perhaps Ashoka sent Buddhist women along with the men on these noble missions in equal measure, thus ensuring the widespread and representative conversion of his populace.

It is unclear whether Ashoka organized the *Dhammayatras* himself or whether they were the effort of his senior Buddhist council. Sri Lankan Buddhist manuscripts suggest that Moggaliputta-Tissa organized missions on Ashoka's behalf in c. 250 BCE to the outer borders of the Mauryan lands. In Ashoka's eighteenth regnal year, nine missions are mentioned as having taken place. Each mission consisted of five monks headed by an elder and included destinations such as Kashmir, Gandhara, Mysore, western India, Sri Lanka, the Greek territories, the Himalayas, and possibly Southeast Asia (lower Burma and Thailand). The only evidence of pilgrimages from Ashoka's edicts was when he visited Lumbini (the birthplace of the Buddha in southern Nepal) and visited the Kanakamuni Stupa in the twentieth year of his reign. Although he invested in the enlargement of this stupa in the fourteenth year of his reign, he erected a pillar at the site to celebrate his visit in c. 249 BCE. However, his Rock Edict XIII explains that he won a "Dhamma Victory" by sending messengers far and wide. Scholars debate whether these were actually Buddhist missions and, more importantly, if the practice of *dhamma* and Buddhism were, in fact, the same thing. Archaeological evidence has been discovered that supports the Buddhist text descriptions of substantial missions, at least in part.

Beyond Ashoka the Great's ascetic work, he was also instrumental in developing infrastructure throughout Maurya. He commissioned roads and waterworks, which facilitated trade and human movement for economic and cultural development. Shade trees, wells, and inns were placed along the roads for weary travelers. Hospitals were established in poor villages, and water sources for the populace were secured through wells and canals. Medicines were provided for humans and animals alike, and medicinal herbs, fruits, and vegetables were grown within the empire or were imported. In keeping with his concept of equality, Ashoka had an open-door rulership style that allowed anybody to approach him at any time with state issues and suggestions. He also personally conducted inspection tours of his realm with his district officers.

In a revolutionary move, Ashoka laid out some of the first vestiges of national environmental policy by protecting the wildlife and all living beings within his realm. Animal sacrifices were outlawed, and the hunting of only certain animals was allowed, with other animals being protected. Ashoka created wildlife preserves and other protected areas to conserve animals and forests. However, not all of his conservation efforts were altruistic. The *Arthashastra* gives an interesting account of the sanctification of elephants for the purposes of breeding and training war elephants, which were crucial to the Mauryan army and one of the main reasons why they enjoyed military success for generations. Chanakya's *Arthashastra* specifies that forests were of critical importance in this respect, as ready supplies of elephants should be kept in designated areas overseen by officials known as "Protectors of the Elephant Forests." This preservation was considered the easiest and cheapest way to capture and train elephants rather than pursuing them through the wild.

This extract from the *Arthashastra* describes some of the specifications for raising tame elephants:

> On the border of the forest, he [the Elephant Official] should establish a forest for elephants guarded by foresters. The Office of the Chief Elephant Forester should with the help of guards protect the elephants in any terrain. The slaying of an elephant is punishable by death.

Besides there being large tracts of protected forests, similar conservation zones were designated for lions and tigers for their skins, although this practice may have been discontinued after Ashoka's conversion. The "Protector of Animals" held off thieves and dangerous predators in other areas to make the woods safe for grazing cattle. The forest tribes (reminiscent of the Kalingas) were never entirely trusted by the Mauryan overlords. When certain forested areas were strategically or economically important, Mauryan officials would bribe or subjugate the border tribes in these areas to their will. The Mauryans employed some members of these tribes to guard borders and trap animals. Although these forested areas were technically part of the Mauryan Empire, they were never completely tamed by the Mauryan authorities, so these alternative methods of creating mutually beneficial relationships enabled Maurya to remain in control and guard their borders. Despite Ashoka's announcements after his conversion that animals were not to be killed, there is evidence that poaching continued. It is difficult to believe that Ashoka's sudden (and possibly wildly unrealistic) ideals for a ban on hunting could be upheld by the common people, even when he clarified his wish with the edicts.

Perhaps Ashoka's most lasting emblems of influence were the Buddhist stupas (meditation mounds). These surviving relics are sepulchral domes made of stone and decorated with Buddhist reliefs. It is not clear exactly what the stupas were used for except as commemorative places for the relics of the Buddhas and Buddhism. However, it is likely that they had a more functional purpose, such as a place of worship and prayer. The interior walls within the stupas have exposed patterns of the wheel of dharma (dharma chakra) and the swastika, which represents the cosmic dance around a fixed center and wards off evil. It is difficult to believe the historical legend in which Ashoka is credited with the creation of 84,000 stupas and viharas around Maurya or that he spread the Buddha's remains among them. What is evident is that he was responsible for building many of these structures throughout Maurya, which, at that time, stretched through most of modern-day India and sections of Nepal, Pakistan, Bangladesh, and Afghanistan. Ashoka apparently chose urban nodes populated by 100,000 people or other noteworthy Buddhist sites. At least twelve substantial Buddhist stupas and viharas in India and Pakistan have been officially attributed to Ashoka.

[9] The Great Stupa (Mahastupa), Sanchi, India, was commissioned by Ashoka the Great. This is not the original stupa, as that would have been made from bricks and been about half the size and surrounded by monasteries in a complex. These stupa complexes evolved over time into what can be seen today, in which there are at least fifty monuments. The Great Stupa is thought to have been rebuilt by Agnimitra, the son of Pushyamitra, the first ruler of the Shunga dynasty who killed the last Mauryan emperor. The religiously intolerant Pushyamitra destroyed many Buddhist shrines and persecuted the monks, but his son attempted to rectify his misdeeds after ascending the throne. The stupa gates were built by the Satavahana dynasty. The surrounding railing and gates are emblematic of stupa constructions.

Ashoka's reign took place about 200 years after the death of Siddhartha Gautama (the Buddha), but one of the Buddha's suggestions had supposedly been that stupas be spread far and wide to provide ordinary people with abundant opportunities to connect to the divine through meditation, which Ashoka took to heart. The above picture of the famous stupa in Sanchi is not an original structure, but it provides an idea of the investment and dedication Ashoka must have had for his faith. Ashoka's most famous surviving stupas are located at Sanchi and Bharhut (both in Madhya Pradesh), Amaravati and Nagarjunakonda (in Andhra Pradesh), and Bodh Gaya (Bihar).

When Ashoka was about fifty-five years old (c. 249 BCE), he undertook his own pilgrimage of Buddha's holy sites, including Lumbini (the supposed birthplace of the Buddha). Other records suggest he took a number of tours during his reign, during which he visited important Buddhist sites, spread the concept of *dhamma*, and performed other social welfare duties. Ashoka's pilgrimages sometimes took years, and he traversed to the southern tip of India and also into foreign lands, such as modern-day Nepal and Greece. However, this may be speculation, as it is more likely that his tours remained within the confines of Maurya while he sent envoys farther afield. His last dated inscription is on Pillar Edict IV from his twenty-sixth regnal year. This would have been around ten years before he died. From then until the end of his life, the only sources of information regarding his history are the Buddhist texts. It was said that his primary queen, Asandhimitra, died during his twenty-ninth regnal year and was replaced three years later by the ascension of his wife Tishyarakshita (possibly the same person as Karuvaki). It is not clear how Ashoka ended his days, but folklore tells that he was extremely ill and was draining the state coffers to make donations to Buddhist priests and monasteries. When he was prevented from doing this, he began giving away his personal possessions to the Buddhist cause until he had nothing left. He died around the age of seventy-two in c. 232 BCE, and he was cremated.

Although the historical records cannot be considered entirely accurate, it is clear that whether saintly or cruel, Ashoka was a force to be reckoned with. It appears that if he set his mind to something, such as conquering previously independent territories or influencing the spirituality of the entire pan-Indian continent and beyond, he always met with success due to his sheer determination and single-mindedness. Although Buddhism is now considered one of the major world religions, it was only a few hundred years old when Ashoka reigned, and it was not established as a major belief system. Ashoka used Buddhism (whether intentionally or not) as more of a sociopolitical instrument than a true mechanism of conversion. As a leader, he was not intent upon converting his people to Buddhism and is widely known to have practiced authentic religious tolerance, going so far as to decorate and donate cave temples to the Ajivikas (the Barabar Caves). Ashoka's support of Buddhism seems to have been more of a suggestion to his people. In this way, he acted as a facilitator for the faith, not a radical religious convertor or maniacal enforcer of a new pervasive religion. Buddhism was still developing, and at times, it seemed to carry more of an intellectual weight than a practical guidance system that could be easily implemented.

During the first nine years of his reign, Ashoka put his considerable energy into conquering new territory, consolidating what he had inherited, and applying the sovereign guidance of his forebears—whether this was a good idea or not. For the remaining twenty-seven years of his rulership, Ashoka the Great put this same considerable energy behind a new way of life in the form of Buddhism. Although the altruistic and non-violent principles of Buddhism were a remarkable and unexpected diversion from the warlike times in which he lived, it is also clear that Ashoka was using an overarching moral and spiritual doctrine to maintain a consolidated economic and political powerbase. After all, he did not give up his army or taxation system, nor did he undermine the thriving trading system that his forebears had promoted.

As an example of Ashoka's contradictory style of rulership, he retained the previously conquered state of Kalinga and did not recall the recorded 150,000 people who had been deported after the war. (Records do not clarify where they were sent or why, but perhaps they posed a threat to his rule.) Ashoka never disbanded his army during his reign, and it is probable that the army was continually used to subdue rebellions. Ashoka continued to rule, even after his advocacy for Buddhism, in accordance with the *Arthashastra*, which promulgated that a strong king must maintain control under any circumstances and by using any means. The *Arthashastra* suggests that a truly wise king will know what is best for all of his people and implement it accordingly. The evidence suggests that Ashoka was aware of these dichotomies but was helpless to retract his actions in Kalinga because it would have made him appear weak or even opened up Maurya to malicious foreign enemies. He strove from that point onward to become a better man and monarch, but at the end of the day, he was still the ruler of the empire and would go to any lengths to keep it that way.

Ashoka's ambitious nature was not reduced when he stopped his conquests, although he already controlled most of the subcontinent. Instead, he used Buddhism to reorganize society so that he could find order in the chaos that generations of warmongering had caused. Ashoka turned to piety, humility, and non-violence in the solace of his post-war years. He not only took it upon himself to foster and preach the gentle ways of Buddhism but also sent emissaries, including his own children, to influence others in all corners of his realm. Ashoka's idealism was genuine, but he was also naïve in thinking that his successors would apply the same balance of power and piety in their rule. After his death, it was clear that his successors and even much of Maurya were not as committed to this new way of life as they may have pretended or visibly adhered to. Ashoka's extraordinary system began to crumble upon his death. He had installed a single, unified, and peaceful vision in a unique moment in history, but unfortunately, his example did not last. After his reign, the Mauryan Empire began to decline.

To close the chapter on Ashoka's history, here is a quotation from the ruler himself: "All men are my children. As for my own children I desire that they may be provided with all the welfare and happiness of this world and of the next, so do I desire for all men as well."

Chapter 7 – The Weakened Empire

From 232 to 185 BCE (about half a century), six more emperors ruled a shrinking Maurya. These men were Dasharatha (r. c. 232-224 BCE), Samprati (r. c. 224- 215 BCE), Shalishuka (r. c. 215- 202 BCE), Devavarman (r. c. 202- 195 BCE), Shatadhanvan (r. c. 195-187 BCE), and Brihadratha (r. c. 187- 185 BCE). All six remaining emperors were considered weak, and after Ashoka's death, the golden age of Maurya ended. Some historians believe Maurya was split into two hemispheres: the western and the eastern. Kunala, Ashoka's son, ruled the western half, and Dasharatha, Ashoka's grandson, ruled the eastern half, which went on to become the final remaining quadrant of the empire, mainly consisting of the greater Magadha kingdom. However, others believe that Ashoka's son Kunala was blinded by his stepmother and could not take over any of Maurya. Ashoka's eldest son Mahinda followed his father into Buddhism, supposedly becoming a Buddhist monk, so he could not rightfully take the throne. Tivara allegedly died before Ashoka, and for some reason, Ashoka's final son, Taluka, was also unable to ascend the throne. Thus, the Mauryan lineage was continued by Ashoka's grandson, Dasharatha.

Legends tell that Dasharatha lost many territories, some of which were regained by Kunala's son, Samprati, the ruler of Maurya after Dasharatha died. The other four rulers of Maurya consistently lost territory. They gave in to stronger territorial leaders such as Sophagasenus of the Hindu Kush and other growing independent states. The top-heavy Mauryan administration, with its micromanagement of the populace and over taxation, could never have lasted for long, especially considering how large the empire had been at its zenith.

Hindu priests intervened to reinstate the caste system, and Hinduism gradually crept back into the empire to replace the Jainism and Buddhism instituted by two of the longest-reigning Mauryan emperors. The Brahmins had lost power and money during Ashoka's installation of Buddhism. The equality of the social classes had limited their power, and Ashoka's dissolution of animal sacrifices meant the Hindu priests could not collect money for these rituals. Evidently, Ashoka's puritanical approach to rulership was not convenient for everybody in Maurya.

At the height of its power, Maurya built a strong market economy through public-private partnerships, taxes, and the collection of wartime plunder. Large private commercial corporations had existed before the rise of the Mauryan Empire, and the emperors wisely allowed them to continue, sometimes leveraging their output or skills for public-private endeavors. The stronger kings of Maurya administered and traded with natural resources, such as timber and salt, as well as manufactured and crafted goods, such as arms and boats. Farming constituted the main activity of the populace, which was taxed. Tradespeople were organized into guilds with executive and judicial authority; these guilds also functioned as banks. The establishment of compulsory market nodes ensured the movement of people as well as goods throughout the Mauryan Empire. A sophisticated Mauryan national economy was built upon the taxes from all goods sold within the confines of the kingdom as well as abroad, and tolls were established on major byways and bridges.

Maurya developed its own coinage in silver, gold, bronze, and copper, but barter was also prevalent. Large capitals, such as Taxila, were permitted to print their own coins. The state tended to fix the price of goods and often intervened to inspect weights and measures. Money was lent on interest using promissory notes, and a single currency system was maintained from Chandragupta's reign, which was based upon Chanakya's *Arthashastra*. The caduceus (three vertical circles intersected with a line) was a monarchical symbol used during the Mauryan era and appears on some of the punch-marked coins. The caduceus may have been Ashoka's personal symbol.

[10] The single currency system (the Karshapana) of Maurya was instituted by Chandragupta Maurya. They used silver punch-marked coins with regional symbols such as elephants and wheels.

The mighty Ganges River and its tributaries carried ships that facilitated trade with the border territories of modern-day China, Sri Lanka, and the empire's main seaports. An ancient highway (the Uttarapatha) ran through the center of Maurya from the capital of Pataliputra to the Indus River in the west and was described by Megasthenes in the *Indika*. This east-west conduit was well sign-posted, patrolled, and occasionally marked by Ashoka's edicts. The Indian subcontinent was linked via extensive and established trade routes through the Indo-Greek kingdoms to the northwest as well as the Malay Peninsula in Southeast Asia. India's main exports were silks, textiles, arms and weaponry, spices, and exotic foods. It is also likely that they traded in minerals, metals, and precious and semi-precious mined materials because Maurya was rich in natural resources. Maurya's investment in infrastructure had helped to increase productivity and economic activity to support this international trade.

Administratively, the emperor (or king) ruled unequivocally but with a board of advisors, who counseled the ruler on matters such as governance, the treasury, and the military. However, the king had ultimate control over the military, executive, and judiciary branches, and he administered Maurya through provinces, each with its own ruling prince and royal court. Maurya's hierarchal civil bureaucracy is similar to modern-day national administrative systems. Evidence suggests that Maurya was highly administered—perhaps too much so—to support the king and keep him politically and economically on top. The people complained of provincial bureaucratic corruption and oppression, and they sometimes rebelled against the Mauryan officials in charge—such as at Taxila during Bindusara's reign. The emperor's control included an extensive spy network and the maintenance of a large army, even once the borders of Maurya were defined. The army continued to draw from the empire's revenue well after the third and final strong emperor, Ashoka, ceased to do battle. Maintaining the salaries and equipment necessary for an army, which was the next biggest sector after farming, without the army adding any further real value to the kingdom may have been one of the factors that led to Maurya's eventual demise.

Ashoka's focus on the spread of Buddhism through Maurya distracted him from military strategies in the northwestern and Greek territories, which grew stronger during his reign. He failed to implement methods that could repel invasions for generations to come. Although he had good relations with the Seleucid Empire along the northwestern border, there were other empires, such as the

Greco-Bactrians, that later took advantage of a relatively demilitarized and fragmented India.

Ashoka's death was the catalyst for the weakening of the border states. Ashoka had been a very involved leader, even evangelizing or sending his children to do so at the far corners of his realm. Maurya had always been too big and complex for one man to rule alone. The integrated governance system and civil structures could only last so long without a more pervasive and integrated objective ruling council or some other system. In addition, the costs of maintaining and defending Maurya were far too high. The governance of this extraordinary kingdom was too unwieldy to be maintained, so local strongholds were established along the major trade routes by local rulers. Leaders of small fiefdoms began diverting money away from the central treasury. The future leaders of the Gupta Empire eventually arose out of these fiefdoms a few centuries later.

After Ashoka's death, quarrels over ascendancy arose, and some southern princes defected. This confusion and disorder encouraged invasions into sections of Maurya and the reassertion of several states to once again rule independently. Naturally, Kalinga was one of these. The kingdom that had experienced a huge setback at the beginning of Ashoka's rule once again rose up, doing so seven years after his death. In 225 BCE, the Chedis (Chetis) were in charge of the Kalinga region, as the Mauryan ruler after Ashoka—Dasharatha—had failed to hold Kalinga. The third Chedi leader, Kharavela, would emerge sometime after the Chedis had achieved dominance. It is believed he was twenty-four when he became the king Kalinga, and he was intent on taking back the kingdom and restoring the pride of his people, who had been subjugated by Ashoka.

Kalinga includes the modern-day state of Odisha (and also some of Andhra Pradesh), whose capital is Bhubaneswar. Near the capital is a Buddhist complex named Udayagiri, which consists of rock-cut Jain temples and viharas. One such cave, the "Elephant Cave" (Hathigumpha), contains a detailed rock inscription of Kharavela's rule. Here, Kharavela credits himself with the reestablishment of the Kingdom of Kalinga during his fourteen-year-long rule. Attributed with regaining independence, fighting off the Greeks, and leading other expeditions and battles, he strangely remains enigmatic today, even though he was the only prominent leader of his time within the region. This royal eulogy attributes Kharavela with regaining the holy Jain idols taken during the Nanda and Mauryan dynasties (particularly after Ashoka's Kalinga War). It also attributes Kharavela, whose exact dates of rulership remain uncertain, with subjugating the rulers of the Shunga dynasty, which ruled after the Mauryan dynasty. He is clearly stated as attacking the Magadhan capital of Pataliputra and making the Shunga king bow at his feet.

Very little is written about the last six Mauryan emperors. Although Dasharatha ruled over a shrinking Maurya, he continued the religious and social policies of his grandfather, Ashoka. He was also the final Mauryan emperor to have contributed to India's edicts, at least according to epigraphical evidence. Since, for some reason (supposedly blindness), the heir presumptive after Ashoka, Kunala, was unable to reign over all of Maurya, the fragmentation of Maurya was imminent. It seems that even with the appointment of Dasharatha, some of the members of the Mauryan royal family set up their own fiefdoms, specifically in the outer regions farther away from the capital of Pataliputra. Classical records indicate that these independent rulers developed their own relationships and arrangements with the Greek world, such as Sophagasenus and Antiochos III in 206 BCE during the reign of Shalishuka. Dasharatha was considered militarily weak, and the more independent states in the south eventually broke away and formed their own sovereignty. According to Jain texts, the provinces of Saurashtra, Maharashtra, Andhra, and Mysore broke away from Maurya soon after Ashoka's death, but they may have been regained by Samprati, Dasharatha's successor.

The familial relationship between Dasharatha and Samprati is not clear. Some texts describe them as cousins coming from different sons of Ashoka. Some texts suggest that they were brothers from one father (most likely Kunala), while other texts suggest that Samprati was actually Dasharatha's son. What is clear is that they were closely related members of the same imperial family. The ruler who followed Samprati, Shalishuka, ruled for about thirteen years and was also believed to have been an adherent of Jainism. The Puranas describe him as being "righteous of speech but unrighteous of action," and he was thought to be quarrelsome. Of the final three emperors—Devavarman, Shatadhanvan, and Brihadratha—virtually nothing is known except that they each reigned for about seven years.

Chapter 8 – Fall of the Mauryan Kingdom: The Shunga Coup

In 185 BCE, the last Mauryan emperor, Brihadratha, was killed by his own general (*Senapati*), Pushyamitra, while inspecting his troops. Pushyamitra went on to found the Shunga (Sunga) dynasty, although, by this stage, Maurya had shrunk to just three city-states—Pataliputra, Ayodhya, and Vidisha. Although the Mauryan Empire had been superbly administered by the first three Mauryan emperors, it was too large, and many regions were inaccessible for official information and governance systems to take hold indefinitely.

The destruction of Maurya had been imminent since the death of the great and beloved Ashoka two generations before. The six weaker Mauryan kings tried to hold onto the disintegrating empire, but their diminished rules allowed the emergence of independently controlled states with their own political ambitions. Ashoka's admirable proselytizing of a "one-size-fits-all" concept of *dhamma*, whereby those born in lowly positions could attain the same spiritual elevation through adherence to a strict moral code as those born in exalted social positions, may not have been as acceptable to those in power, as they most likely preferred a more hierarchical system in which they had more influence.

The Brahmin Shunga general Pushyamitra, who was said to have cold-bloodedly dispatched the final Mauryan emperor, was known to be religiously intolerant and has been accused of destroying Buddhist monasteries and stupas, including the Great Stupa in Sanchi. He reintroduced animal sacrifices and persecuted Buddhist monks as far as modern-day Pakistan, according to the 4th-century CE Buddhist manuscript *Divyavadana*. Pushyamitra was a strong supporter of orthodox Hinduism, but his son, Agnimitra, attempted to undo some of the damage created by his father when he ascended the throne. However, many historians do not believe that Buddhists were persecuted during the Shunga dynasty, or at least not after Pushyamitra's rule.

The Shunga dynasty continued to rule for over a century in the central Indian subcontinent, mostly around the Magadha region. The Shunga capital was Pataliputra, although Vidisha became a capital as well later on, which was located more in the center of the northern subcontinent. In 73 BCE, they were replaced by the Kanva dynasty.

The disintegration of Maurya left the subcontinent vulnerable along its northwestern borders, specifically the famous Khyber Pass (Pakistan/Afghanistan border), which had been used by conquerors over the centuries to annex India. Greco-Bactrian King Demetrius I (r. c. 200– 180 BCE), also known as Dharmamitra to the Indians, conquered parts of southern Afghanistan during his rule, as well as large sections of Pakistan and some of northwestern India, forming the Indo-Greek Kingdom. Numismatic evidence points to Demetrius having his capital at Taxila and dominating the northwestern territories, while the Shunga dynasty occupied the Indo-Gangetic Plain. Unique coinage printed by the Indo-Greeks, supposedly around the time of the fall of the Mauryan Empire, points to the Greeks having a more than casual control of the border states in northern Gandhara.

Demetrius later sent two armies deep into India, apparently to complete the capture of the subcontinent where Alexander had failed. Demetrius was taking advantage of the confusion in the north after the collapse of the Mauryan Empire. Other sources suggest that the last emperor of Maurya, Brihadratha, married a daughter of Demetrius named Berenice and that the Greco-Bactrian king's invasion of northern India was to protect his Greek subjects who occupied the subcontinent. However, one of the most interesting historical suggestions is that Buddhism had flourished amongst the Indo-Greek rulers as a result of Ashoka's influence on Maurya and beyond. Some sources indicate that Demetrius invaded the subcontinent to show support for the vanquished Mauryan Empire and in response to the threat on Buddhism with the rise of the religiously intolerant Shunga ruler Pushyamitra. Regardless, it is likely that the motives were not entirely for conquest and economic and territorial gain. The Indo-Greeks retained their hold on the previous trans-Indus Mauryan territories for over a century and continued military forays into the continent. Finally, in approximately 70 BCE, Indo-Scythian (Syria/Iran) tribes overran the Greeks and settled in the trans-Indus valleys and the regions of Gujarat and Mathura (north and northwest subcontinent).

It is possible that the Greek armies got as far as the capital of Pataliputra, but they failed to invade India past that point, as they were pushed back to Mathura (north-central subcontinent). This invasion occurred several years after the fall of Maurya during the Shunga dynasty, but interestingly, Kharavela of Kalinga is credited with repelling the Indo-Greek invasion based on interpretations by historians from his rock edict at the Hathigumpha cave at Udayagiri. Kharavela seems to have been expedient and successful in extending his lands in all directions, and the Hathigumpha inscription suggests he attacked Magadha more than once. On one of these occasions (of which repelling Demetrius was probably the first), the edict reports that he recaptured the Jina—a sacred artifact of the Jain faith that had been taken in prior generations. There is a suggestion that the

Kalingas never appreciated the installation of Buddhism by Ashoka, and Kharavela describes with pride how the Jina was brought back to Kalinga.

Kharavela and his family were also responsible for the establishment of Jain monuments and sacred complexes, such as Udayagiri and Khandagiri. There is evidence that he hosted Jain councils at the sacred caves and temples. After the twelfth year of his reign, Kharavela is thought to have become very devoted to the spiritual Jain life. It is interesting how so many of India's ancient rulers embraced spirituality and asceticism after conquering large swathes of the continent, displacing people, and laying waste to generations. It seems they felt a divine prerogative to do both! This unusual attitude of using warfare to create peace and spiritual tolerance is confirmed by Kharavela's final inscription at the sacred Jain caves.

Kharavela's final installment on the Udayagiri hill stone inscription:

He is the king of peace, of prosperity, of the monks and of the teaching. He is accomplished in extraordinary virtues, respects every sect and repairs all shrines. His armies cannot be vanquished and he protects the realm. He is descended from the family of the royal sage, Vasu.

Like the Jainist Chandragupta Maurya, Kharavela may have completely turned toward the ascetic life before he handed over power because there is no mention of him after he was thirty-eight. After Kharavela's son's rule, the Chedis are not mentioned again.

Controversially, Ashoka the Great is sometimes attributed with contributing to the downfall of the Mauryan Empire. His extraordinarily high ideals and expectations of unity and peace were admirable but unrealistic unless a leader of his unique stature had followed him. Although his *dhamma mahamattas* (*dhamma* ministers) were appointed and instructed to spread the concept of "rightness" through *dhamma*, they were rumored to have created their own power structure in certain instances and interfered with politics. Ashoka's edicts were an earnest attempt to solve the problems of a complex society, but in a sense, it is probable that he became overly focused on a single sector of government to the detriment of others. Although Maurya was incredibly wealthy, Ashoka was intent upon spreading Buddhism rather than developing international relations and trade routes for purely economic purposes. He was not as rigorous at collecting taxes as his forebears had been, and he would not resort to violent measures and bullying to fill the state coffers. To compound this oversight, he maintained an army that was not technically in use, invested heavily in spiritual monuments, and gave generously to Buddhist causes and individuals. Although well intentioned, this single-faceted style of rulership (which may have been compensating for his own personal issues with *dhamma* after the conquest of Kalinga) did not support the kind of heterogeneous powerbase that was required to keep a mega-culture like Maurya in existence. Ashoka's faith in future generations to uphold his altruism and belief systems was too high, and while his contribution to history is remarkable and admirable, he didn't focus on mechanisms and governance systems that may have kept order and peace after his death.

Ashoka's policy of an open, transparent, and approachable government that favored equality and peace over wealth and power struggles did not appeal to everybody. His charity-centered approach was not conducive to the violent and rigorous methods that his ancestors (and even himself) had used to gain and retain Maurya. There may have been some relief when he died, and the previous might of Maurya could have been reestablished, but this was not to be. In an era of conquest and expanding dominions through violent battle, Ashoka was a paragon of his time, but his empire was also unlikely to exist far beyond his passing. This is an extract from one of his edicts that summarizes his altered and enduring attitude to the cessation of war:

This inscription of Dhamma has been engraved so that any sons or great sons that I may have should not think of gaining new conquests, and in whatever victories they may gain should be satisfied with patience and light punishment. They should only consider conquest by Dhamma to be a true conquest, and delight in Dhamma should be their whole delight, for this is of value in both this world and the next.

Chapter 9 – The Remnants of Maurya

Although the accuracy and details of the Mauryan Empire remain obscure and contradictory, the Mauryan emperors and their feats have become legends in Indian history and remain a profound source of inspiration for their culture and governance. Jain records suggest that after his abdication, Chandragupta Maurya moved with a group of wandering Jain monks south to Karnataka, where he renounced his throne and gave up his worldly possessions. At Karnataka, he lived at Shravanabelagola as an ascetic for several years before taking his own life in ritual starvation (*sallekhana*). The hill upon which Chandragupta is said to have lived as a monk is known as Chandragiri Hill, upon which a monument—the Chandragupta basadi (a Jain temple)—stands, amongst other basadis.

[11] Chandragiri Hill Temple Complex at Shravanabelagola, Karnataka, is said to be the location of Chandragupta's last years as an ascetic Jain monk.

Jain legends state that a prominent monk named Acharya Bhadrabahu predicted a twelve-year drought and famine (which, according to scientific records, did occur) and journeyed south with a group of disciples, which included Chandragupta Maurya. Bhadrabahu was considered the last *Sruta Kevali* (an ascetic with complete knowledge of the Jain scriptures) and is attributed with writing the *Niryuktis*, *Samhitas*, and *Kalpa Sutra*. Shravanabelagola is more than 2,000 kilometers (around 1,240 miles) away from Pataliputra, and it is likely that there is some truth in the connection between the location of Chandragiri Hill, Jainism, and Chandragupta.

The fifth emperor of Maurya, Samprati (Ashoka's grandson), was also a Jain, and he is recorded as rectifying many of the misnomers of his predecessor, Dasharatha. Samprati, the son of Ashoka's blind son Kunala, seemed to have been influenced like his grandfather by monks, except they were Jain monks. Similar to his grandfather, Samprati sent Jain missionaries abroad to spread the belief system of Jainism and went so far as to disguise some of his soldiers as Jain monks to reconquer the Mauryan territory lost by his cousin, Dasharatha. Legends say that Samprati's grandmother, Padmavati (Ashoka's wife), was also a Jain. Once Samprati was fully converted, he is recorded as making inroads in converting a large tract of eastern India to Jainism. He continued his Jain missions throughout India and abroad. Samprati somehow ensured the safety of monks traveling to foreign lands and was purportedly responsible for building 125,000 Jain temples (Derasars) and establishing umpteen idols, some of which are still being found today, mostly across southern India. Ancient Jain literature refers to the piousness of Samprati and his many good deeds in support of the religion. Samprati's messengers, like his grandfather's envoys before him, were sent as far afield as Greece, Persia (Iran), and the Middle East. There are currently over four million Jains living in India.

Just north of Pataliputra, at the Barabar Hill Caves, are some of the oldest surviving carved caves in India. The four caves at Barabar (c. 250 BCE) are adjacent (1.6 kilometers—less than a mile—away) to the three Nagarjuni rock-cut chambers (c. 230 BCE). The Barabar chambers bear the name of "King Piyadasi" and date back to Ashoka's reign. Similarly, the Nagarjuni caves bear the name "Dasharatha Maurya," Ashoka's grandson. The sculptured arch of the Lomas Rishi Cave is the earliest example of the chaitya arch (horseshoe-shaped arch) and is also home to the first known Maurya relief, dating from Ashoka's reign. The caves were dedicated to the Ajivikas. The Ajivikas, a separate and atheist sect that no longer exists, had connections to both Buddhism and Jainism. Most of the caves at Barabar consist of two chambers with interesting echo effects. The caves are carved out of granite, and their internal surfaces have the well-known Mauryan polish with a dark, reflective surface.

[12] The entrance to Lomas Rishi Cave at Barabar Hills Caves, Bihar, India, dated to approximately 250 BCE.

Inscription on the Gopika Cave of the Nagarjuni Caves:

> The cave of Gopika, a refuge that will last as long as the sun and the moon, was dug by Devanampiya [Beloved-of-the-Gods] Dasharatha during his elevation to the throne, to make it an hermitage for the most pious Ajivikas.

With the mixing of cultures during the 4th and 3rd centuries BCE, the Mauryan architectural style that was cast in sandstone looks distinctly more Persian (specifically the Achaemenid Empire) than Indian. Contemporary Roman writers who visited India described the Indian palaces as being superior to those of Persia, which was known to be exquisite and was also more documented. As an example, a pillar capital that was discovered from Ashoka's reign in Pataliputra clearly demonstrates the blending of Indo-Bactrian (northern Afghanistan or northern Hindu-Kush) and Indo-Parthian (Iranian) cultures with the Indian culture. Ashoka the Great is attributed with constructing architectural designs in stone rather than wood, possibly as a result of Alexander the Great's influence, who brought in Hellenistic stone architecture. Ashoka's monolithic pillars, which stand forty to fifty feet high, are polished, and foreigners visiting the land described them as "shining like mirrors." This is a particularly impressive example of Mauryan technological and artistic abilities. Most notably, however, Ashoka put most of his creative effort into the establishment of his edicts and holy sites, as well as into the development of the capital of Pataliputra. This development is evidenced by the surviving edicts (specifically the pillars), as well as the stupas and other Buddhist ruins throughout the Mauryan Empire.

[13] The capital (top) of a pillar from Pataliputra (the Mauryan capital city in Magadha—modern-day Patna in Bihar) from the time of Ashoka's reign in the 3rd century BCE. Evidence of a stone-pillared hall is also from this time.

For over 400 years after the death of Alexander, the northwest Indian subcontinent remained heavily influenced and sometimes occupied by the Greeks or their contemporaries. The rule of the Indo-Greeks continued from Alexander's time through the Seleucid Empire and into the 1st century CE. Thirty-six Indo-Greek rulers have been identified through coinage alone. The Indo-Greek rulers continued to send ambassadors into the courts of the Indian mainland, and a broad corridor of cross-cultures emerged across the north of the subcontinent and spread deeper into Greek territory. Indo-Greek coins depicting Hindu gods dating to the time of the fall of the Mauryan kingdom have been found in Afghanistan; they have been attributed to the Bactrian ruler King Agathocles.

The Greeks, and even the Romans who came after, were mesmerized by the exotic "land that lay over the river Indus." Some of the earliest Greek explorers were dispatched circa 600 BCE to explore the Indus River Valley and document their findings for the Western world. From that time onward, many writers, diplomats, and philosophers were dispatched to India, and although most of their writings have been lost, they were often paraphrased in other classical writings so their knowledge could be passed down through the years. The Greek historian Herodotus (5th century BCE) described the great wealth of India, saying that it was "the most populous nation in the world." It is no wonder that it was attractive, both as a place to be conquered and explored, by the Indo-Greeks. Alexander the Great was said to have been so enamored with a flock of peacocks on the banks of the Indus River that he threatened his troops into protecting them. He is thought to have returned home with more than 200 of the birds and distributed them far and wide to the wonder of others.

Maurya existed during the era of Northern Black Polished Ware pottery (NBPW) (c. 700–200 BCE). This was a cultural period marked by several artisanal developments corresponding to significant increases in urbanization. Socioeconomically, this period naturally led to the emergence of India's first large, fortified cities, as well as rapid population growth and increased social stratification. Trade networks grew organically during the NBPW cultural period, specifically around specialized craft industries. Carved ivory, prepared semi-precious stones, diamonds, pearls, prepared cloths, iron-mongering, and forged tools all became part of an advancing basis for trade using specified weights and measures as well as standard currencies. The Black Polished Ware pottery was a form of burnished pottery with an exterior black luster, which was used by the upper classes. It was a luxury item, elegant and refined, and is evidence of the extraordinary craftsmanship of the era. The methods by which the black external polish was created are still not known. The discoveries of NBPW in central and northern India correspond to the spread of Ashoka's empire and simultaneously reflect the spread of Buddhism. The discovery of this Black Polished Ware creates a remarkably similar map of the extent of Maurya.

The Mauryan Empire also existed during a time when writing and epigraphy (written inscriptions) was burgeoning. These written artifacts have provided sources that give historians insight into this unique and astounding period in Indian history. Ashoka's edicts provide some of the earliest evidence of writing in India. Instead of the common Sanskrit, which was typical for the time, Ashoka used local dialects that could be understood by the common people, even using Greek and Aramaic in the northwestern regions. Ashoka's inscriptions are some of the oldest surviving writings in India, and his work began a tradition of epigraphical inscriptions in the subcontinent that lasted for millennia.

By comparing sources, it has been possible to piece together an approximately accurate chronology of the events and rules that defined Maurya. Along with the excavated archaeological evidence and Ashoka's edicts, indigenous literature, spiritual texts, and foreign writings provide sufficient evidence of a fascinating Mauryan lineage that reached an extraordinarily long and peaceful golden age during the thirty-six year-long rule of Ashoka the Great. In an era of constant warmongering and territorial expansion and domination, the reality that the Mauryan Empire held strong—and thrived—for almost a century and a half is remarkable.

Ashoka's *dhammavijaya* (spiritual conquests) supposedly extended far into other lands. Besides being instrumental in the spread of Buddhism to central Asia and North Africa, Ashoka is believed to have sent emissaries (possibly Buddhists) into the northwestern

Seleucid Empire and into the Hellenistic regions of the Mediterranean. With the assistance of the established trade routes—the precursors to the Silk Road—Buddhism eventually spread, giving rise to Greco-Buddhism. Under the Indo-Greeks, Buddhism flourished, and several of their emperors, such as Menander I, became famous adherents of the faith. The *Mahavamsa* refers to an emissary of Ashokan Buddhism—Dharmaraksita—as having been in charge of Greek (*Yavana*) Buddhist monks active in proselytism. The affiliation between these two cultures is evidenced in coinage, reliefs, and other art. However, it was the Kushan Empire (greater Afghanistan) that was principally responsible for the spread of Buddhism to the East, specifically China, in the Common Era, which was mostly spread through the influence of trade and the Silk Road.

Ashoka's influence in countries such as Egypt, Sri Lanka, Burma, Syria, Libya, Macedonia, and Greece resulted in Buddhist monasteries that may have been the inspiration for later Christian monasteries. Ashoka's extraordinarily high ideals and his efforts to build peace and proselytize (not only Buddhism but also essential humanity) laid a foundation for goodness that eventually spread through half the world. Although his ideals were not upheld for long in India, Ashoka's influence was widespread and lasting. Many of the current symbols of India and its national regalia—the wheel, the lions, and the peacock—are thought to have originated during, or at least been inspired by, the Mauryan period. The spoked wheel—or Ashoka Chakra—represents the wheel of *dhamma* set in motion by the Gautama Buddha (the endless cycle of birth and rebirth known as *samsara*) and is part of the flag of modern India. The seal of India contains the lions that appear on Ashoka's capitals.

Ashoka also instituted the revolutionary method of inscribing public messages on stones, which would last through the ages. It is likely that more perishable methods, such as messages on wood and cloth, would have existed as well, but they have disappeared in the sands of time. Ashoka was not only responsible for building schools and monasteries but also ensured the publication of Buddhist literature throughout his realm. Historical records by foreign travelers (such as the Chinese pilgrim Xuanzang) indicate that there were far more pillars than have been discovered to date. The absence of major pillar edicts in the main centers of Pataliputra, Vidisha, Ujjain, and Taxila suggest that these have been lost or destroyed during urbanization. Ashoka's edicts united Maurya in a shared ethic of virtue during his peaceful and extraordinarily long rule. His principles of peace, brotherhood, and gentleness seemed to be more effective than the warmongering of his contemporaries. Since Ashoka continued to maintain such a strong hold on the Mauryan Empire despite his moral and spiritual promulgations, it can be said that he used religion as a political strategy. This great emperor achieved unification through advising "right action" to his people and applied a live-and-let-live attitude while leading by example. He not only practiced what he preached but also toured his lands to spread his message.

The Mauryan Empire heralded a unique time when a multitude of religious and spiritual practices existed simultaneously to create a multifarious fabric of belief systems. Besides making a substantial attempt to create a national moral code and ensure the spiritual protection of his people, Ashoka was a vanguard in instituting socioeconomic reforms, providing necessary civil infrastructure, and preserving the natural environment and wildlife. He was so far ahead of his time that it is difficult to find a leader even in modern times who has achieved a similar status of altruism. Ashoka's profound influence on India through his role as the longest-reigning Mauryan emperor was almost lost. His pillars lay broken and covered by sand, and his edicts ignored as unimportant, with grass and plants covering his stupas and monasteries—those that still stood at least. For almost 700 years since the end of the Middle Kingdom of India, Ashoka and the Mauryan Empire had been forgotten. Once uncovered, the legendary names that appeared in the Puranas and other religious works could, at last, be linked to archaeological evidence. As a ruler like no other,

Ashoka was the only known leader of the ancient world who gave up warfare and conquest at the height of his power and instead preached communal understanding and harmony both in Maurya and abroad.

At its height, the Mauryan Empire consisted of most of southern Asia (or the entirety of the Indian subcontinent), and it remains to this day the largest single political entity of the subcontinent. During most of its 137-year existence, it was a thriving hub of industry, trade, agriculture, religion, and culture. The Mauryans created the Grand Trunk Road (Uttarapatha or the "Northern Road"), one of Asia's most established and longest trade routes that linked the entirety of the northern subcontinent. Chandragupta Maurya is attributed with building this highway, which was in use for two and a half millennia. Although Chandragupta's original road was about 2,600 kilometers (1,615 miles), successive empires continued to contribute to the road until it reached a length of almost 4,000 kilometers (almost 2,500 miles), running from modern-day Afghanistan in the west to the border of Myanmar in the east. Ashoka added improvements to the Uttarapatha in his time.

Although the Silk Road lay north of the Indian subcontinent and was only prevalent just after the death of Ashoka, Ashoka's spread of Buddhism would have intersected and cross-pollinated along trade routes that joined the Silk Road to India. This intermingling of cultures and religions enabled the spread of Buddhism into Eastern and Southeast Asia. Ashoka's work has been known to have increased the popularity of Buddhism in Afghanistan, Thailand, and northern Asia, including Siberia. Even countries that were not directly on the Silk Trade routes are known to have been heavily influenced by the civilizations that connected the trade network, such as the Indian subcontinent—and the influence was reciprocal. From the 4th century CE onward, Asian pilgrims traveled along the Silk Road, as well as the Mauryan Northern Highway, in search of original Buddhist scriptures and to visit the holy Buddhist sites. Such pilgrims included the Chinese Buddhist translator and writer Fa-hsien, whose pilgrimage to

India took place between 395 and 414 CE; the priest and scholar Xuanzang, who was also a Buddhist monk; and Hyecho, a student of esoteric Buddhism who traveled from Korea. Ashoka's lasting influence on Asian Buddhism cannot be dismissed, but it was done within the context of the Mauryan Empire as a whole. He could not have had the impact he had on the religion without being the Mauryan emperor, whose geopolitical reach, wealth, and infrastructure provided the platform he needed to gain traction in spreading his belief system. Also, Ashoka was not the only one who influenced a religious revival in Asia. Chandragupta's late adoption of Jainism led to religious reforms across south Asia, where Jainism is still practiced to this day.

The Mauryan Empire existed as a dichotomous kingdom. Potential oppressors feared their military might and the dominance they had over the untamed wildernesses of the vast geographical expanse of India. What is known about the most prominent Mauryan emperors is that they valued mighty warfare and conquest just as highly as spiritual sovereignty and religious asceticism (although not necessarily at the same time). The Western world was very aware of this contradiction, as Megasthenes described the Mauryans as "freedom-loving," but it was simultaneously evident that the Seleucid Empire was wise enough to maintain friendly relations rather than face the might of Maurya in an invasion. The remarkable historical figures of the Mauryan dynasty are known for their rampant ambition and absolute adherence to a sovereign form of government on their terms, for better or for worse. The visionary accomplishments of the first three Mauryan emperors and the infamous consort of the first two emperors—Chanakya—suggest that the ends might have justified the means. However, it was Ashoka's legendary epiphany that violence should not be the way but rather peaceful negotiation within the boundaries of military might and political domination that may have proved otherwise. For almost three decades after Ashoka renounced warfare, he ruled over a peaceful and fully intact Maurya. Perhaps his strategy of *dhamma* was the correct one to apply, but perhaps he was also just fortunate that his forebears had handed him a mighty conquered kingdom and all the resources to institute whatever policy he saw fit—peaceful or otherwise. The disintegration of Maurya during successive generations after Ashoka suggests that he led Maurya during its golden age and that no matter the policies he instituted, such a mega-culture was destined to eventually collapse.

Conclusion

The rise of Maurya saw the development of a pan-Indian empire that required allegiance to a central monarchy rather than the loyalties to kin and tribal regions that had been prevalent before. The title of an all-powerful king became a hereditary privilege. In an era that lacked an established, independent, and objective government, the strength of the empire depended upon the strength of the king. Maurya can attribute much of its longevity to its first three kings. Their reigns were long (stretching from approximately twenty-four to thirty-six years each), and they held or extended the limits of the empire, investing heavily in trade, infrastructure, and the people.

Chandragupta Maurya is heralded as a visionary leader and the founder of one of the greatest empires the world has ever known. He seized power at a pivotal point in India's history and was perfectly positioned to take advantage of the power vacuum that Alexander the Great had left in the northwestern subcontinent. Even more advantageous for him was the wide unpopularity of the Nanda Empire and the confusion and fragmentation that the withdrawal of the Macedonian troops had left.

The Mauryan Empire was one of the largest empires in world history. Along with the Gupta Empire, these unified kingdoms used consolidation as the basis for their political and economic strength. The first Mauryan emperors secured the borders of their realm through warfare and later by strategic diplomacy and even peaceful spirituality.

Similar to modern-day national systems, Maurya organized a central bureaucratic authority to govern and collect taxes. However, this centralized but all-pervasive government was not only a top-down hierarchy. The Mauryan Empire—particularly during the reign of Ashoka the Great—ensured ancient social security systems and support for the poorest and most marginalized members of the Mauryan population.

Maurya existed for almost one and a half centuries, and its emperors practiced religious tolerance, socioeconomic upliftment, and the development of arts and culture. This civilization reached its zenith during the extended rule of Ashoka the Great, who preached love for humankind, freedom from suffering, and even the prevention of cruelty to animals. Although Maurya was founded upon bloody warfare and political maneuvering, half a century into its existence, the kingdom had perhaps achieved the vision held by its founders, Chandragupta Maurya and his chief advisor Chanakya—that of an extensive and centrally controlled mega-culture.

Perhaps Maurya was only able to exist because of the groundwork Alexander had laid when he subjugated much of the northwestern stretches of the dominion. Perhaps the first three rulers of Maurya were simply lucky in their timing and positioning, and perhaps the intimidation of the Indian war elephant was simply too much for the average battle-weary soldier to face. But a dynasty lasting almost 150 years is not established or continued on luck alone. The sheer geographical expansiveness of Maurya, as well as abundant evidence of sophisticated economic, trade, civil, and social systems, suggest it was an empire that knew exactly what it was doing and why. Much of the evidence, both archaeological and apocryphal, is contested, and while the overall Mauryan story is commonly accepted, it is likely that new discoveries will considerably alter its history as we currently understand it. We will never know the true intentions of some of the

Mauryan emperors, but we can enjoy the historical gifts left by the Mauryan Empire, such as religious structures and official edicts, as well as sculptures, art, and the records of international relations and cross-border marriages. Maurya reaches across time as one of the largest and most intriguing empires of its era and suggests that there is so much more to be understood.

Here's another book by Captivating History that you might like

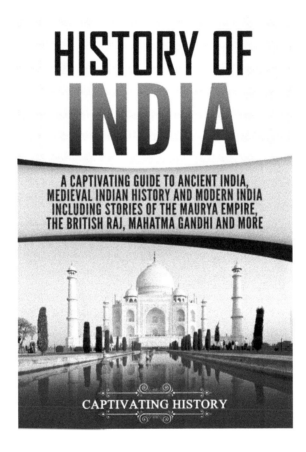

Free Bonus from Captivating History
(Available for a Limited time)

Hi History Lovers!

Now you have a chance to join our exclusive history list so you can get your first history ebook for free as well as discounts and a potential to get more history books for free! Simply visit the link below to join.

Captivatinghistory.com/ebook

Also, make sure to follow us on Facebook, Twitter and Youtube by searching for Captivating History.

References

Ancient Buddhist Texts:

- Malalasekera, G.P., 1937. Reprinted by the Pali Text Society, Oxford, 1988. For the Variants: Geiger, W., 1908. Reprinted by the Pali Text Society, Oxford, 1958. Translated by Bhikkhu, Anandajoti, 2012. *The Extended Mahavamsa, Asoka and the Missions*, accessed via Ancient Buddhist Texts, *Introduction*, https://www.ancient-buddhist-texts.net/Texts-and-Translations/Asokan-Missions/00-Introduction.htm, accessed November, December 2020.

- *Asoka's Edicts*, https://www.ancient-buddhist-texts.net/Maps/During-Asokas-Time/Map-11-Asokan-Edicts.htm, accessed November, December 2020.

- *Northern Black Polished Ware (7th-2nd centuries BC)*, https://www.ancient-buddhist-texts.net/Maps/During-Asokas-Time/Map-14-7-NBPW.htm, accessed November, December 2020.

Ancient History Encyclopedia:

- Basu, Anindita, 2016. *Mauryan Empire*, https://www.ancient.eu/Mauryan_Empire/, accessed November, December 2020.

- Lal, Dr Avantika, 2019. *Chandragupta Maurya*, https://www.ancient.eu/Chandragupta_Maurya/, accessed November, December 2020.

- Mark, Joshua J., 2020. *Ashoka the Great*, https://www.ancient.eu/Ashoka_the_Great/, accessed November, December 2020.

- Mark, Joshua J., 2020. *Chanakya*, https://www.ancient.eu/Kautilya/, accessed November, December 2020.

- Sanujit, 2011. *Cultural links between India & the Greco-Roman world*, https://www.ancient.eu/article/208/cultural-links-between-india--the-greco-roman-worl/, accessed November, December 2020.

Angel Education, YouTube, *The Mauryan Dynasty (History) in English*, https://www.youtube.com/watch?v=mzte8p36kII, December 2017, accessed November, December 2020.

Britannica:

- *Artha-shastra work by Chanakya*, https://www.britannica.com/topic/Artha-shastra, accessed November, December 2020.

- *Bindusara Mauryan Emperor*, https://www.britannica.com/biography/Bindusara, accessed November, December 2020.

- *Mauryan Empire ancient State, India*, https://www.britannica.com/place/Mauryan-Empire, accessed November, December 2020.

Dhammika, Ven. S, 1993. *The Edicts of King Ashoka: an English Rendering (The Wheel Publication No. 386/387)*, https://www.cs.colostate.edu/~malaiya/ashoka.html, Colorado State University, College of Natural Sciences, accessed November, December 2020.

History's Histories, *India The Mauryan Empire,*
http://www.historyshistories.com/india-mauryan-empire.html,
accessed November, December 2020.

The Indian Express:

- Beg, Sahil M., 2020. *How Seleucus I Nicator gave away
  most of Pakistan and Afghanistan for 500 elephants,*
  https://indianexpress.com/article/research/seleucus-nicator-
  chandragupta-maurya-india-greece-6466470/, accessed
  November, December 2020.

- *The Largest City in the World and other fabulous Mauryan
  Facts,* updated 2019.
  https://indianexpress.com/article/parenting/learning/world-
  largest-city-mauryan-facts-5542516/, accessed November,
  December 2020.

Jagran Prakashan Limited (JPL) Publishers, "Education Web Portal",
https://www.jagranjosh.com/:

- Jagran Josh, 2015. *Foreign Invasions during Pre Mauryan
  Age,* https://www.jagranjosh.com/general-knowledge/foreign-
  invasions-during-pre-mauryan-age-1437215972-1, accessed
  November, December 2020.

- Jagran Josh, 2015. *Magadhan Empire,*
  https://www.jagranjosh.com/general-knowledge/magadhan-
  empire-1437397156-1, accessed November, December 2020.

- Jagran Josh, 2015. *Ashoka the Great,*
  https://www.jagranjosh.com/general-knowledge/ashoka-the-
  great-1437043068-1, accessed November, December 2020.

- Jagran Josh, 2015. *Economy, Social Life, Art and
  Architecture in Mauryan Age,*
  https://www.jagranjosh.com/general-knowledge/economy-
  social-life-art-and-architecture-in-mauryan-age-1437216944-1,
  accessed November, December 2020.

- Jagran Josh, 2015. *Mauryan Dynasty,* https://www.jagranjosh.com/general-knowledge/mauryan-dynasty-1437043587-1, accessed November, December 2020.

- Jagran Josh, 2015. *Mauryan Empire: Its Decline and Significance,* https://www.jagranjosh.com/general-knowledge/mauryan-empire-its-decline-and-significance-1437458920-1, accessed November, December 2020.

- Jagran Josh, 2015. *The Mauryan Empire: Administration,* https://www.jagranjosh.com/general-knowledge/the-mauryan-empire-administration-1437217258-1, accessed November, December 2020.

- Jagran Josh, 2015. *Sunga, Kanva, and Chedi Dynasty,* https://www.jagranjosh.com/general-knowledge/sunga-kanva-and-chedi-dynasty-1437397149-1, accessed November, December 2020.

- Jagran Josh, 2017. *Janapadas and Mahajanapadas,* https://www.jagranjosh.com/general-knowledge/janapadas-and-mahajanapadas-1437458526-1, accessed November, December 2020.

- Jagran Josh, 2017. *Sources of Mauryan History,* https://www.jagranjosh.com/general-knowledge/sources-of-mauryan-history-1436957802-1, accessed November, December 2020.

The Khan Academy:

- Shelby, Dr. Karen. *The Pillars of Ashoka,* accessed via the Khan Academy https://www.khanacademy.org/humanities/art-asia/south-asia/x97ec695a:art-magadha/a/the-pillars-of-ashoka, November, December 2020.

- *The Maurya and Gupta Empires,* https://www.khanacademy.org/humanities/world-history/ancient-medieval/early-indian-empires/a/the-maurya-and-gupta-empires, accessed November, December 2020.

- *The rise of empires in India,* video, https://www.khanacademy.org/humanities/world-history/ancient-medieval/early-indian-empires/v/chandragupta-ashoka-and-the-maurya-empire, accessed November, December 2020.

- *The Stupa,* https://www.khanacademy.org/humanities/ap-art-history/introduction-cultures-religions-apah/buddhism-apah/a/the-stupa, accessed November, December 2020.

Knowledgia, YouTube, *Why did the Mauryan Empire Collapse?,* *https://www.youtube.com/watch?v=DSof2HncHvo,* October 2018, accessed November, December 2020.

Live History India (LHI):

- Haraniya, Krutika, 2017. *The Greek Connection,* https://www.livehistoryindia.com/forgotten-treasures/2017/06/07/the-greek-connection, accessed November, December 2020.

- Jain, Anshika, 2019. *Shravanabelagola & Its Mauryan Connection,* https://www.livehistoryindia.com/amazing-india/2019/07/04/shravanabelagola-its-mauryan-connection, accessed November, December 2020.

- LHI Team, 2019. *How the Ancient West saw India,* https://www.livehistoryindia.com/cover-story/2019/09/07/how-the-ancient-west-saw-india, accessed November, December 2020.

- LHI Team, 2020. *India's Earliest Kings (6th BCE – 1st BCE),* https://www.livehistoryindia.com/history-daily/2020/05/21/indias-earliest-kings, accessed November, December 2020.

- LHI Team, 2020. *Sanchi, A Canvas of Buddhist History,* Video, https://www.livehistoryindia.com/tales-and-trails/2020/01/15/sanchi-a-canvas-of-buddhist-history, accessed November, December 2020.

- Menon, Mini, 2019. *Chandragupta Maurya: Emperor to Ascetic (324-297 BCE),* https://www.livehistoryindia.com/history-of-india-2000-years/2019/12/17/chandragupta-maurya-emperor-to-ascetic-324-297-bce, accessed November, December 2020.

- Menon, Mini, 2020. *Kalinga Before Ashoka (7ᵗʰ BCE - 3ᵈ BCE),* https://www.livehistoryindia.com/history-of-india-2000-years/2020/01/12/kalinga-before-ashoka-7th-bce-3rd-bce, accessed November, December 2020.

- Menon, Mini, 2020. *Kalinga's King Kharavela (2ⁿᵈ BCE – 1ˢᵗ BCE),* https://www.livehistoryindia.com/history-of-india-2000-years/2020/04/05/kalingas-king-kharavela-2nd-bce-1st-bce, accessed November, December 2020.

- Shah, Aditi, 2019. *Pataliputra: Destroyed but Not Doomed,* https://www.livehistoryindia.com/history-of-india-2000-years/2020/01/18/ashoka-from-guilty-to-great-269-bce-232-bce, accessed November, December 2020.

- Shah, Aditi, 2020. *Ashoka: From Guilty to Great (269 BCE – 232 BCE),* https://www.livehistoryindia.com/history-of-india-2000-years/2020/01/18/ashoka-from-guilty-to-great-269-bce-232-bce, accessed November, December 2020.

- Shah, Aditi, 2020. *Peacock: A Constant in Indian Culture,* https://www.livehistoryindia.com/history-daily/2020/01/20/peacock-a-constant-in-indian-culture, accessed November, December 2020

- Shah, Aditi, 2020. *Sarnath, Where Buddha Spoke,* https://www.livehistoryindia.com/amazing-india/2020/05/04/sarnath, accessed November, December 2020.

The Indian Monk, YouTube, https://www.youtube.com/watch?v=Nu0Rt1Z7_K4, *The History of the Mauryan Empire in India,* September 2019, accessed November, December 2020.

MrDowlingdotcom, video, *Ashoka and the Mauryan Empire,* https://youtu.be/-2u00ynvYdQ, accessed November, December 2020 via History's Histories, *India The Mauryan Empire.*

National Geographic Society:

- Rattini, Kristin Baird, 2019. *Who was Ashoka?,* https://www.nationalgeographic.com/culture/people/reference/ashoka/#close, accessed November, December 2020.

- *Mauryan Empire,* https://www.nationalgeographic.org/encyclopedia/mauryan-empire/, accessed November, December 2020.

New Word Encyclopedia:

- *Kautilya,* https://www.newworldencyclopedia.org/entry/kautilya, accessed November, December 2020.

UNESCO (United Nations Educational, Scientific, and Cultural Organization), *Shahbazgarhi Rock Edicts,* https://whc.unesco.org/en/tentativelists/1880/, accessed November, December 2020.

Wikipedia:

- *Alexander the Great,* https://en.wikipedia.org/wiki/Alexander_the_Great, accessed November, December 2020.

- *Ashoka,* https://en.wikipedia.org/wiki/Ashoka, accessed November, December 2020.

- *Ashoka's Policy of Dhamma,*
https://en.wikipedia.org/wiki/Ashoka's_policy_of_Dhamma,
accessed November, December 2020.

- *Barabar Caves,* https://en.wikipedia.org/wiki/Barabar_Caves,
accessed November, December 2020.

- *Bindusara,* https://en.wikipedia.org/wiki/Bindusara, accessed
November, December 2020.

- *Brahmin,* https://en.wikipedia.org/wiki/Brahmin, accessed
November, December 2020.

- *Buddhism,* https://en.wikipedia.org/wiki/Buddhism,
accessed November, December 2020.

- *Chanakya,* https://en.wikipedia.org/wiki/Chanakya, accessed
November, December 2020.

- *Chandragupta Maurya,*
https://en.wikipedia.org/wiki/Chandragupta_Maurya, accessed
November, December 2020.

- *Dasharatha Maurya,*
https://en.wikipedia.org/wiki/Dasharatha_Maurya, accessed
November, December 2020.

- *Demetrius I of Bactria,*
https://en.wikipedia.org/wiki/Demetrius_I_of_Bactria,
accessed November, December 2020.

- *Edicts of Ashoka,*
https://en.wikipedia.org/wiki/Edicts_of_Ashoka, accessed
November, December 2020.

- *Grand Trunk Road,*
https://en.wikipedia.org/wiki/Grand_Trunk_Road, accessed
November, December, 2020.

- *Maurya Empire,* https://en.wikipedia.org/wiki/Maurya_Empire, accessed November, December 2020.

- *Nanda Empire,* https://en.wikipedia.org/wiki/Nanda_Empire, accessed November, December 2020.

- *Pataliputra,* https://en.wikipedia.org/wiki/Pataliputra, accessed November, December 2020.

- *Pillars of Ashoka,* https://en.wikipedia.org/wiki/Pillars_of_Ashoka, accessed November, December 2020.

- *Puranas,* https://en.wikipedia.org/wiki/Puranas, accessed November, December 2020.

- *Northern Black Polished Ware,* https://en.wikipedia.org/wiki/Northern_Black_Polished_Ware, accessed November, December 2020.

- *Samprati,* https://en.wikipedia.org/wiki/Samprati, accessed November, December 2020.

- *The Seleucid Empire,* https://en.wikipedia.org/wiki/Seleucid_Empire, accessed November, December 2020.

- *Seleucid-Mauryan War,* http://en.wikipedia.org/wiki/Seleucid-Mauryan_war, accessed November, December 2020.

- *Shalishuka,* https://en.wikipedia.org/wiki/Shalishuka, accessed November, December 2020.

- *Silk Road,* https://en.wikipedia.org/wiki/Silk_Road, accessed November, December 2020.

- *Tamils,* https://en.wikipedia.org/wiki/Tamils, accessed November, December 2020.

- *Vajrasana, Bodh Gaya,*
https://en.wikipedia.org/wiki/Vajrasana,_Bodh_Gaya, accessed
November, December 2020.

Image References

[1] Artist's impression of Chanakya, 1915. *Source*: Wikipedia, *Chanakya*, https://en.wikipedia.org/wiki/Chanakya, accessed November, December 2020.

[2] Statue of Chandragupta Maurya. *Source:* Violatti, Christian, 2013. Accessed via Ancient History Encyclopedia, *Statue of Mauryan Emperor Chandragupta,* https://www.ancient.eu/image/2125/statue-of-mauryan-emperor-chandragupta/, accessed November, December 2020.

[3] Maurya c. 250 BCE, 2014. *Source*: Wikimedia Commons, By Avantiputra7 - Own work, CC BY-SA 3.0, https://commons.wikimedia.org/w/index.php?curid=33663725, accessed November, December 2020.

[4] Ashoka the Great. *Source*: indiaonline, https://www.indiaonline.in/about/personalities/historicalheroes/ashoka, accessed November, December 2020.

[5] Maurya Map, 265 BCE. *Source:* keeby101, 2014, accessed via Ancient History Encyclopedia, *Mauryan Empire,* https://www.ancient.eu/Mauryan_Empire/, accessed November, December 2020.

[6] Ashoka Relief. *Source*: Wikipedia, *Ashoka*, https://en.wikipedia.org/wiki/Ashoka, accessed November, December 2020.

[7] Ashoka Rock Edict, Shahbazgarhi. *Source*: Wikimedia Commons, franek2, 2003, https://web.archive.org/web/20161020134256/http://www.panoramio.com/photo/50089833, accessed November, December 2020.

[8] Edicts of Ashoka. *Source:* History's Histories, http://www.historyshistories.com/india-mauryan-empire.html, accessed November, December 2020.

[9] The Great Stupa. *Source:* Nagarjun, Kandukuru, 2011, *Great stupa of Sanchi*, https://www.flickr.com/photos/nagarjun/6370232595/in/photolist-aGV7dt-aGV9Qv-bguZ3i-biVsFX-a715wJ-eWFGgB-biVtaa/, accessed via The Khan Academy, November 2020.

[10] Silver punch mark coins. *Source*: New World Encyclopedia, *Kautilya*, https://www.newworldencyclopedia.org/entry/kautilya, accessed November, December 2020.

[11] Chandragiri hill temple complex at Shravanabelagola, 2008. *Source*: Wikimedia Commons, By Dineshkannambadi at English Wikipedia, CC BY-SA 3.0, https://commons.wikimedia.org/w/index.php?curid=4371178, accessed November, December 2020.

[12] Lomas Rishi Cave. *Source*: Photo Dharma, 2018. Accessed via Wikimedia Commons, https://en.wikipedia.org/wiki/File:Lomas_Rishi_entrance.jpg, November, December 2020.

[13] Pataliputra Capital. *Source*: Wikipedia, *Ashoka*, https://en.wikipedia.org/wiki/Ashoka, accessed November, December 2020.